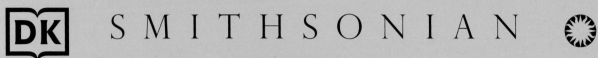

SMITHSONIAN

Everything you need to know about
BUGS

Written and edited by Caroline Bingham,
Ben Morgan, Matthew Robertson
Designed by Tory Gordon-Harris, Karen Hood
Editorial assistance Fleur Star
Design assistance Gemma Fletcher, Sadie Thomas
DTP design Ben Hung
Illustrator Mark Beech
Production Claire Pearson
Picture research Liz Moore
Jacket designer Hedi Gutt

Publishing manager Susan Leonard
Art director Rachael Foster
Category publisher Mary Ling
Creative director Jane Bull

Consultants Matthew Robertson, Derek Harvey

THIS EDITION
Senior editor Shaila Brown
Senior art editor Smiljka Surla
Jacket design development manager Sophia M. T. T.
Jacket designer Laura Brim
Jacket editor Maud Whatley
Producer, Pre-production Adam Stoneham
Producer Mary Slater
Managing editor Paula Regan
Managing art editor Owen Peyton Jones
Publisher Sarah Larter
Associate publishing director Liz Wheeler
Art director Phil Ormerod
Publishing director Jonathan Metcalf

DK Delhi
Senior editor Anita Kakar
Senior art editor Mahua Sharma
Project art editor Vaibhav Rastogi
Art editor Parul Gambhir
DTP designer Jaypal Chauhan
Managing editor Rohan Sinha
Managing art editor Sudakshina Basu
Production manager Pankaj Sharma
DTP manager Balwant Singh

This abridged American Edition, 2015
First American Edition, 2007 as *Buzz*
Published in the United States by DK Publishing
1745 Broadway, 20th Floor, New York, NY 10019

DK books are available at special discounts when purchased in bulk
for sales promotions, premiums, fund-raising, or educational use.
For details, contact: DK Publishing Special Markets,
1745 Broadway, 20th Floor, New York, NY 10019
SpecialSales@dk.com.

Printed and bound in China

www.dk.com

Smithsonian Institution
This trademark is owned by the Smithsonian Institution and
is registered in the United States Patent and Trademark Office.

Consultant: Smithsonian's National Zoo
Alan Peters, Curator
Mike Henley, Biologist
Tamsen DeWitt, Animal Keeper
Pamela Baker-Masson, Director, Communications
Jennifer Zoon, Communications Assistant

Established in 1846, the Smithsonian Institution—the
world's largest museum and research complex—includes
19 museums and galleries and the National Zoological Park.
The total number of objects, works of art, and specimens
in the Smithsonian's collection is estimated at 137 million.
The Smithsonian is a renowned research center, dedicated
to public education, national service, and scholarship
in the arts, sciences, and history.

Buzzz

CONTENTS

400 million years ago (or thereabouts), the ancient ancestors of today's **insects**, **millipedes**, and **spiders** were at home on land rather than among life in the sea. They were the **FIRST ANIMALS** to walk on land. Another 398 million years were to pass before **humans** arrived. If all the world's humans and *all other* large animals were to disappear, the tiny creepy-crawlies that share our planet would get on with life without a second thought.

But if *they* disappeared, our world would collapse. With no bees and bugs to pollinate **flowers**, crops would fail and we would **starve**. With NO beetles and flies to recycle our waste, dead bodies and *dung* would pile up all over the place. The little creatures that **crawl** around our gardens, **creep** across our ceilings, and **buzz** around our lives are MORE than *important*. **They are** essential. Without them, the world would be a very **nasty** place indeed.

ARTHROPOD
= "*jointed foot*"

Insects, **spiders**, and other *creepy-crawlies* make up a **group** of animals known as THE **ARTHROPODS**. The word *arthropod* means **"jointed foot,"** and that's what all these **animals** have: tiny legs **made of** little **struts** with *bendable* joints.

Black widow spider

Arthropods can also have…

- body and legs divided into segments
- body separated into head, thorax, and abdomen, but thorax and abdomen may be fused together
- many undergo metamorphosis from young to adult forms
- a life span of just a few weeks to well over a hundred years
- bodies as small as a grain of salt or as big as a shark (… fortunately that one is extinct!)

Ladybug

The most important feature that *all arthropods* share is this: THEIR BODIES ARE INSIDE OUT. Most big animals, such as cats and dogs and human beings, have a skeleton on the inside. An arthropod has hard skin that is like a skeleton *on the outside*. Like a suit of armor, the external skeleton (or *exoskeleton*) is made of stiff plates linked together. Between the plates are flexible joints that let the body move.

The exoskeleton is the secret of the arthropod's success because it holds all the animal's organs and keeps its insides from drying out. In addition, all sorts of different structures have evolved—from claws and jaws to wings and stings. **But there's a catch!** External skeletons cannot grow with the body, so arthropods have to shed them and *make new ones* to grow BIGGER.

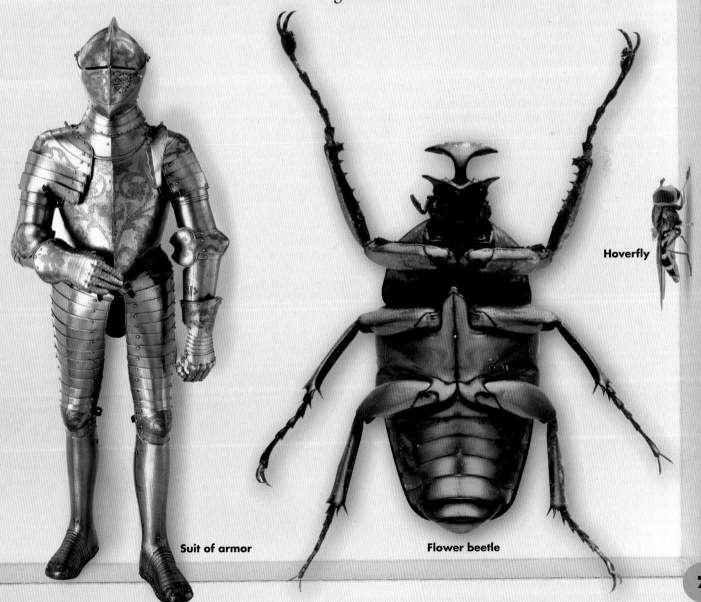

Hoverfly

Suit of armor

Flower beetle

Long legs, short legs, fat legs, thin legs, hairy legs, smooth legs, prickly legs, soft legs, strong

HOW MANY

6

Weevil

Crane fly

6 legs
Probably an insect. Insects are the most successful land animals on Earth. Most have six legs, a pair of antennae (feelers) at the front, two pairs of wings, and a body divided into three segments: a head, a thorax (chest), and an abdomen (belly).

8 legs
Probably an arachnid. Spiders, scorpions, ticks, and mites are all arachnids. Unlike insects, arachnids never have wings or antennae, and their bodies are divided into only two segments. Most of them are flesh eaters.

Tarantula

8

10

LEGS?

There are probably millions of different arthropods, so how do you tell them apart? Here's a clue: **count the legs**. Most arthropods belong to one of four major categories, and the number of legs is a good clue to the right category.

10 legs
Probably a crustacean. Crabs, lobsters, crayfish, and shrimp are all crustaceans. Most crustaceans live in water and breathe through gills. Not all have 10 legs though—they can have dozens or none at all. Wood lice are crustaceans that live on land, and they have 14 legs each.

Crab

Lots of legs
Probably a centipede or a millipede. These arthropods have long thin bodies divided into lots of segments, with legs on each segment. *Centipede* means "a hundred feet" and *millipede* means "a thousand feet," but, in fact, the number of legs can be anything from 30 to 750.

Centipede

Millipede

30+

0 legs

No legs
Probably a slug, a snail, a worm, or even the larva of an arthropod (like a maggot). These slippery creatures aren't arthropods. They have no jointed legs and no external skeleton. Slugs and snails do have feet though, but only one—a single giant foot all the way along the body.

Slug

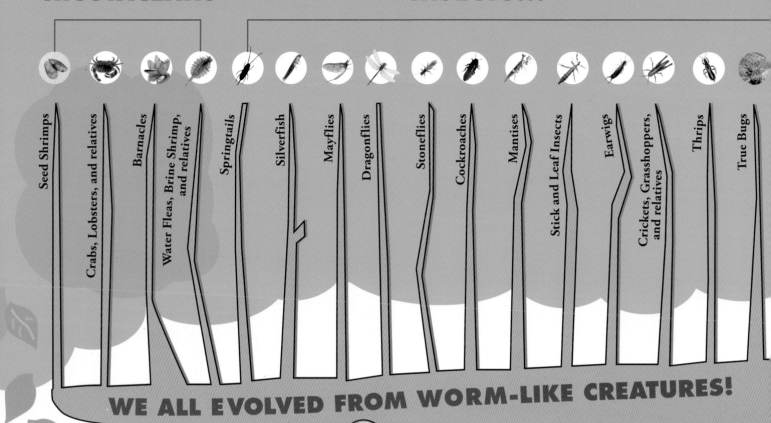

Seed Shrimps

Crabs, Lobsters, and relatives

Barnacles

Water Fleas, Brine Shrimp, and relatives

Springtails

Silverfish

Mayflies

Dragonflies

Stoneflies

Cockroaches

Mantises

Stick and Leaf Insects

Earwigs

Crickets, Grasshoppers, and relatives

Thrips

True Bugs

WE ALL EVOLVED FROM WORM-LIKE CREATURES!

Meet the
family

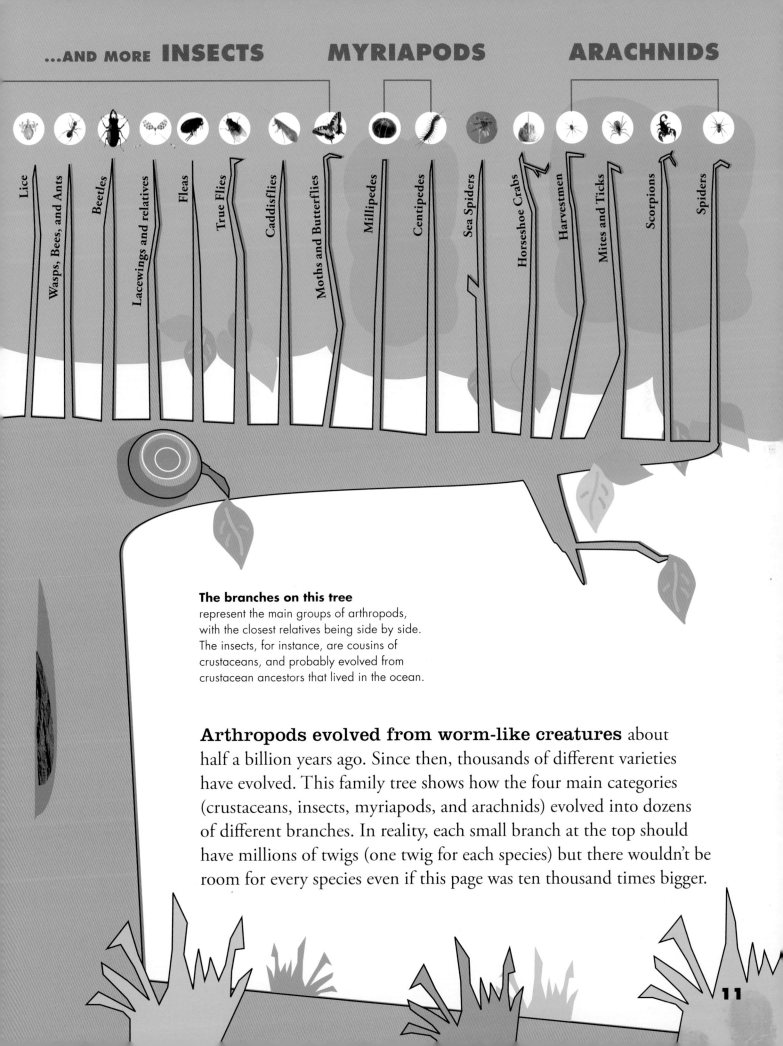

Lice

Wasps, Bees, and Ants

Beetles

Lacewings and relatives

Fleas

True Flies

Caddisflies

Moths and Butterflies

Millipedes

Centipedes

Sea Spiders

Horseshoe Crabs

Harvestmen

Mites and Ticks

Scorpions

Spiders

The branches on this tree
represent the main groups of arthropods,
with the closest relatives being side by side.
The insects, for instance, are cousins of
crustaceans, and probably evolved from
crustacean ancestors that lived in the ocean.

Arthropods evolved from worm-like creatures about half a billion years ago. Since then, thousands of different varieties have evolved. This family tree shows how the four main categories (crustaceans, insects, myriapods, and arachnids) evolved into dozens of different branches. In reality, each small branch at the top should have millions of twigs (one twig for each species) but there wouldn't be room for every species even if this page was ten thousand times bigger.

If you shared the world's land evenly among the number of species, arthropods would get every continent and island except South America.

WHO RULES THE WORLD?

At least **90%**

Arthropods are the most successful animals on Earth. They've conquered *land*, *sea*, and *air* and live everywhere from the depths of the oceans to the tops of mountains. Scientists have so far discovered and named more than 1.6 million different types, or species, of animal. About

of animal species on Earth are **ARTHROPODS**

nine out of 10 of these—more than a million in total—are arthropods.

But those are just the species that have been cataloged. There are countless more waiting to be discovered. Around 25 new arthropod species are discovered **every day**, and there's currently a 15-year backlog of newly discovered species waiting to be officially named and described. So the true number of arthropod species alive is anybody's guess, but it's probably **millions**.

Insects are the **biggest** group of arthropods by far, with more than a million named species.

According to one expert, the total number of individual insects alive on Earth is 120 million billion. In other words…

…for **every person** alive today, there are *200 million* **insects**.

How arthropods conquered

540 MYA

Our story starts 540 million years ago (MYA), when there was little life on Earth besides microbes and worms on the seabed. Some of the worms evolved external skeletons, and their segments sprouted legs—they became **arthropods**. Soon, these new creatures would conquer the world.

1st TO RULE THE SEA

358 MYA

Lush **forests** spread across the land during the Carboniferous Period. Towering trees provided new habitats for animals, but only for those that could reach them. So having conquered land and sea, the arthropods took to the air...

1st TO WALK ON LAND

520 MYA

Within a few million years, arthropods were scuttling all over the seafloor like huge wood lice. These were **trilobites**—the most successful animals of their day. They ruled the seas for nearly 300 million years. Their tough skeletons formed millions of fossils that are easy to find, even today.

438–408 MYA

Prehistoric arthropods grew to gigantic sizes. The biggest were probably **Eurypterids**—scorpion-like sea creatures that reached 13 ft (4 m) long (as big as a crocodile). Their tails were tipped with a vicious spike that may have been used to inject venom.

350 MYA

By 350 million years ago, land arthropods had evolved into giants, too. Millipedes grew to 7 ft (2 m) long and scorpions were 3 ft (1 m) long—as big as a dog.

428 MYA

428 million years ago, arthropods began to conquer the land. **Millipedes** about ½ in (1 cm) long became the first animals ever to walk on our planet.

320 MYA

The **first flying animals** were insects. They looked like a cross between mayflies and cockroaches and had either four or six beautifully patterned wings. Insects remained the only flying animals on Earth until 100 million years later, when pterosaurs evolved.

505 MYA

Millions of years before sharks evolved, arthropods were the top predators in the sea. The trilobites' number one enemy was probably **Anomalocaris**, a monstrous, shrimplike creature that was bigger than a man and had gigantic claws at the front for snatching trilobites. It was the great white shark of its day.

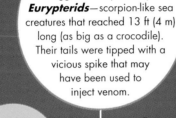

300 MYA

Silverfish— slithering silvery insects with no wings—appeared 300 million years ago and have barely changed since.

PRECAMBRIAN   CAMBRIAN   ORDOVICIAN   SILURIAN   DEVONIAN   CARBONIFEROUS

600 million years ago (MYA)   **500**   **400**   **300**

the world...

How do we know?

Everything we know about the history of arthropods comes from fossils—the remains of ancient animals preserved in rock. The best insect fossils are found in amber, a honey-colored rock formed from the sticky sap of pine trees. Even insects trapped in amber 100 million years ago look as if they died only yesterday, with legs and wings perfectly intact. Thanks to amber, we know that all the main types of insect were here on Earth 90 million years ago.

40-million-year-old fossilized fly in amber

1st IN THE AIR

280 MYA

By 280 million years ago, even the flying insects had become giants. The skies were ruled by dragonfly-like creatures called **griffen flies**, which swooped about on 30 in (75 cm) wingspans.

220-209 MYA

Wasps appeared in the late Triassic Period. The first wasps were small, solitary insects. Later, wasps began to form colonies.

140 MYA

The first **fleas** probably sucked the blood of dinosaurs. Later, they adapted to live off of birds and mammals as well.

145-133 MYA

Ants appeared about 140 million years ago. They evolved from social wasps that had given up flying.

92-73 MYA

Butterflies appeared in the late Cretaceous. They evolved from moths.

230 MYA

Beetles appeared in the Triassic, about the same time as the first dinosaurs.

Dinosaurs first appeared about now.

207-188 MYA

Moths appeared in the early Jurassic Period.

And finally...

Modern human beings didn't show up on Earth until about 100,000 years ago. That means arthropods have been here five thousand times longer than us.

PERMIAN **TRIASSIC** **JURASSIC** **CRETACEOUS** **CENOZOIC**

200   100   NOW

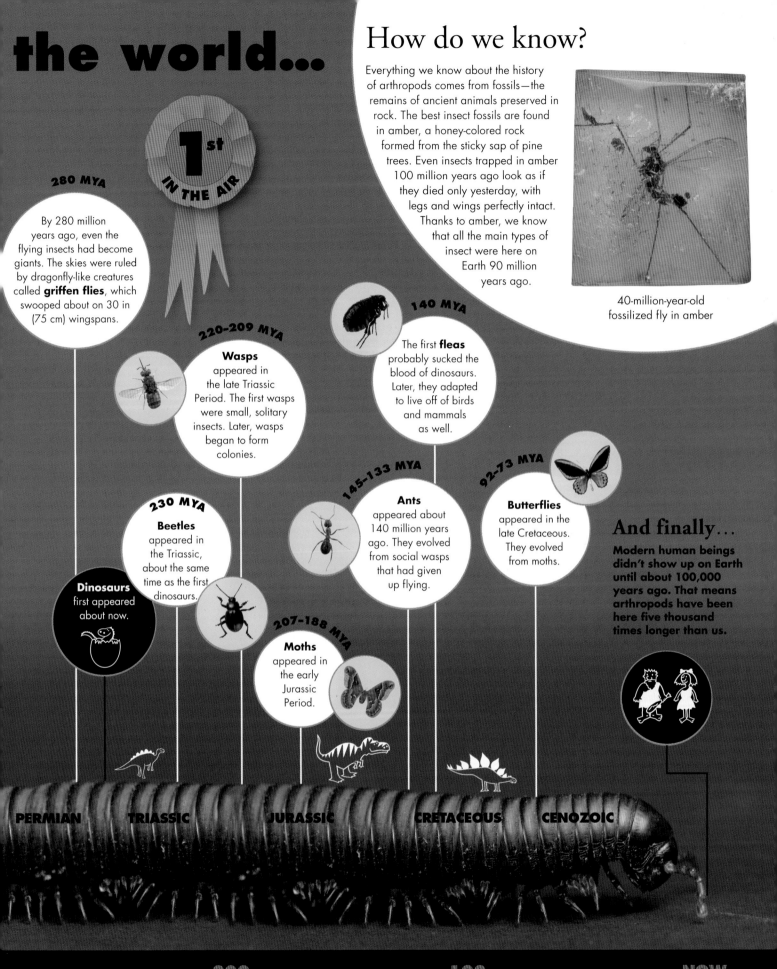

What is an insect?

Insects are the most successful and common of all the arthropods. In fact, they are so common that lots of people say "insect" when they actually mean "arthropod." The secret of the insects' success is their ability to fly, which allowed the very earliest insects to flee from enemies and conquer new habitats. Today's insects all share certain key features that were passed down from those distant ancestors. Typically, adult insects have six legs, two pairs of wings, and a body divided into three main sections: the head, the thorax (chest), and the abdomen (belly).

Hoverfly

Walking
Insects typically walk by moving three legs forward at once, then the other three, and so on. As a result, there are always at least three legs touching the ground at once, forming a triangle—the most stable type of shape. Six is the minimum number of legs needed to keep arthropod bodies stable. The arrangement works so well that it is copied in robots.

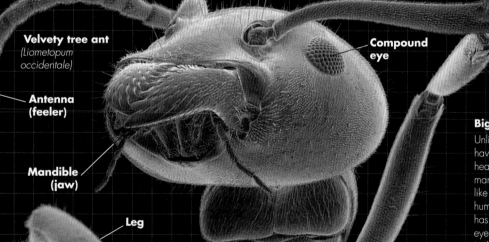

Velvety tree ant
(Liometopum occidentale)

Antenna (feeler)

Mandible (jaw)

Leg

Compound eye

Big mouth
Unlike most other arthropods, insects have mouthparts that are outside their heads. The large jaws (called mandibles) of this ant work sideways like shears—the opposite of how human jaws work. The ant also has a single pair of compound eyes and a single pair of feelers (called antennae). These are typical features of insects, too.

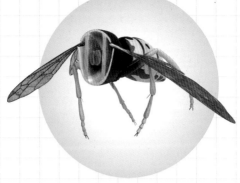

Flight muscles
In some insects the flight muscles pull on the base of the wings, but in others, such as this wasp, they pull on the wall of the thorax. This produces a faster wing beat.

Head
As with most animals, an insect's head is where the main sense organs, mouth, and brain are. The antennae not only feel objects but smell and taste them, too. The compound eyes are made of hundreds of separate eyes packed together.

Thorax
The thorax is where all the legs and wings attach. Inside it are powerful flight muscles. Most insects have two pairs of wings that beat together, but dragonflies beat theirs alternately. Flies use only one pair of wings, giving superb maneuverability—they can fly backward or even upside down.

Abdomen
The back end of an insect contains the main parts of its digestive system, the heart (which is tube-shaped), and the sex organs. Some female insects have an egg-laying tube at the rear; in bees and wasps this tube is also the stinger. There are no true legs on the abdomen, but caterpillar abdomens have false legs.

German wasp (*Vespula germanica*)

Compound eye

Antenna

Hairy body

Claw

Seen close-up, many insects are surprisingly hairy. The hairs help keep the flight muscles warm. Hairs on the legs also double as sense organs that can feel and taste whatever they touch.

WINGS & THINGS

Vein

Membrane

Insect wings are hugely **important**, both to insects and to people. Why? They help *insects* to escape, find food, and find and attract a mate. They help *people* to separate different insects into groups.

Let's LOOK at a **wing**

All insect wings are made up of thin membranes supported by a network of tiny veins. However, there are so many differences between different types of insect wing that entomologists use these differences to name some groups of winged insect.

What *kind* of *wing*?

The Greek word **pteron** means "fin," "wing," or "feather." When used for insects, it means "wing." There are lots of insect groups, but some of the largest are the **Coleoptera**, or "sheath-winged" insects, the **Hymenoptera**, or "membranous-winged" insects, the **Diptera**, or "two-winged" insects, and the **Lepidoptera**, or "scale-winged" insects. Then there are the **Orthoptera**, with "straight wings," and the **Neuroptera** with their "nerve wings."

"So, what am I?"

"You're a Hymenopteran."

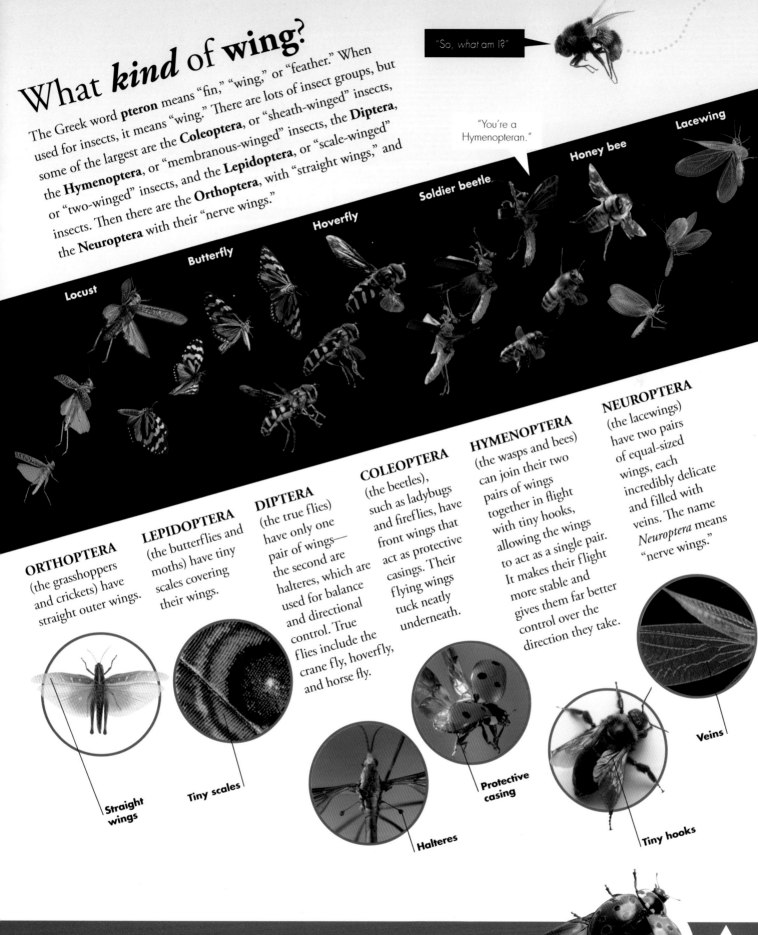

Lacewing

Honey bee

Soldier beetle

Hoverfly

Butterfly

Locust

ORTHOPTERA
(the grasshoppers and crickets) have straight outer wings.

LEPIDOPTERA
(the butterflies and moths) have tiny scales covering their wings.

DIPTERA
(the true flies) have only one pair of wings—the second are halteres, which are used for balance and directional control. True flies include the crane fly, hoverfly, and horse fly.

COLEOPTERA
(the beetles), such as ladybugs and fireflies, have front wings that act as protective casings. Their flying wings tuck neatly underneath.

HYMENOPTERA
(the wasps and bees) can join their two pairs of wings together in flight with tiny hooks, allowing the wings to act as a single pair. It makes their flight more stable and gives them far better control over the direction they take.

NEUROPTERA
(the lacewings) have two pairs of equal-sized wings, each incredibly delicate and filled with veins. The name *Neuroptera* means "nerve wings."

Straight wings

Tiny scales

Haltères

Protective casing

Tiny hooks

Veins

Insects have to warm up their flight muscles before they take off. A beetle will often open and shut its wing cases a few times to do this.

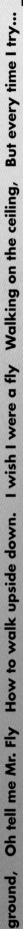

UPSIDE DOWN

Have you ever watched a fly or another insect walking up the wall and then along the ceiling? Don't you wish you could do that too? Just how do they manage to defeat the laws of gravity?

x 100

Did you know?
Houseflies spend their whole lives in the same area; they don't move far from their place of birth.

x 1,000

A housefly has two claws on the end of each foot. Under these are two sticky pads, each covered with minute hairs. The hairs produce a gluelike substance.

So a fly effectively "glues" itself to the ceiling. The claws help it to push its leg off the ceiling. (It is because of these sticky pads and its hairy legs that the housefly is a carrier of all kinds of nasty diseases and germs.)

So how does a fly LAND on the ceiling? The fly does not fly upside down. Just before it lands the fly stretches its front legs over its head to reach the surface. It then hauls its body around in a kind of somersault to bring the remaining four legs into contact with the ceiling. Touchdown!

Watch closely and you may see a fly twist as it "unglues" itself before moving on. A fly always keeps four feet on the ceiling.

"unglue" itself? Give a little twist... give a little push... and it takes to the air! As a fly walks across the ceiling, it leaves behind

a trail of sticky footprints. Can it get stuck to the ceiling? No. It uses its tiny claws to push itself

What's inside an insect?

An insect's skeleton is on the outside of its body rather than the inside. If we looked inside our own bodies, we would find our organs surrounded and held together by our bones. So what happens inside an insect's body?

Let's look at a locust

Like people, insects have to eat, process food, breathe, carry blood, and sense the surrounding world with their organs. It's a lot to fit inside a tiny body!

Brainbox
The brain is the insect's control center. It lies behind the eye.

Crop
Food is stored in a stretchy bag called a crop.

Heart
An insect's tubular heart runs along the upper part of its body. The heart pumps blood around the body.

Ganglion
A ganglion is a dense collection of nerve cells. Insects have several. This one controls the mouth.

Gizzard
In some insects, the gizzard grinds up the food a little more than the stomach does.

Ovaries
Fertilized eggs pass through an egg-laying tube and are laid in soft, damp soil.

Nervous system
Nerve centers are attached to the nerve cord. They send messages to the muscles.

Grasshoppers, crickets, and locusts are grouped in the same order of insects: Orthoptera. There are thousands of different species—at least 20,000 different grasshoppers and crickets alone. Below is just a small selection!

Locust

Grasshopper

Grasshopper

Grasshopper

Locust

Grasshopper

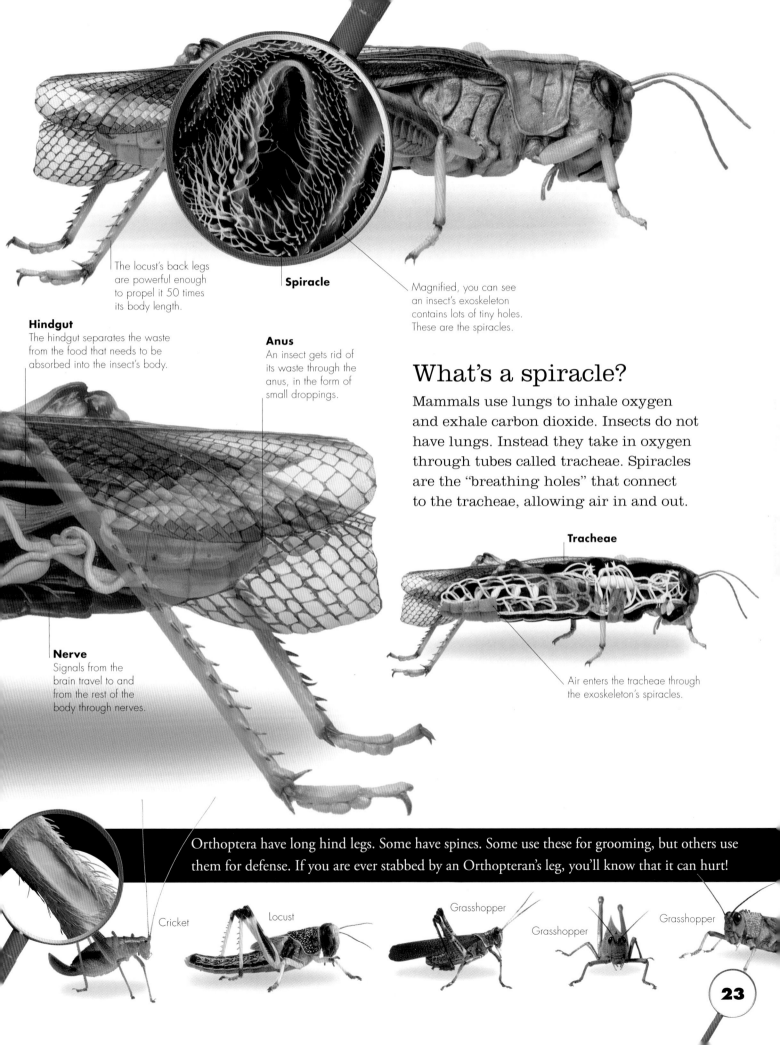

The locust's back legs are powerful enough to propel it 50 times its body length.

Spiracle

Magnified, you can see an insect's exoskeleton contains lots of tiny holes. These are the spiracles.

Hindgut
The hindgut separates the waste from the food that needs to be absorbed into the insect's body.

Anus
An insect gets rid of its waste through the anus, in the form of small droppings.

What's a spiracle?

Mammals use lungs to inhale oxygen and exhale carbon dioxide. Insects do not have lungs. Instead they take in oxygen through tubes called tracheae. Spiracles are the "breathing holes" that connect to the tracheae, allowing air in and out.

Tracheae

Air enters the tracheae through the exoskeleton's spiracles.

Nerve
Signals from the brain travel to and from the rest of the body through nerves.

Orthoptera have long hind legs. Some have spines. Some use these for grooming, but others use them for defense. If you are ever stabbed by an Orthopteran's leg, you'll know that it can hurt!

Cricket

Locust

Grasshopper

Grasshopper

Grasshopper

eye
SEE things
you *wouldn't believe!*

How many eyes does an insect have?

Insects' compound eyes aren't as good as ours. If we had compound eyes, they'd need to be 50 times bigger than human eyes to produce our normal quality of vision.

Many insects have two eyes, but believe it or not, a lot of insects have five! A honeybee, for example, has two multi-surface, compound eyes as well as three simple eyes (or "ocelli"). So do a grasshopper and a dragonfly. The simple eyes help these insects detect light and movement. The compound eyes allow them to see the world in detail.

INSECTS DON'T HAVE EYELIDS. THEY RUB THEIR

WHAT DO THEY SEE?

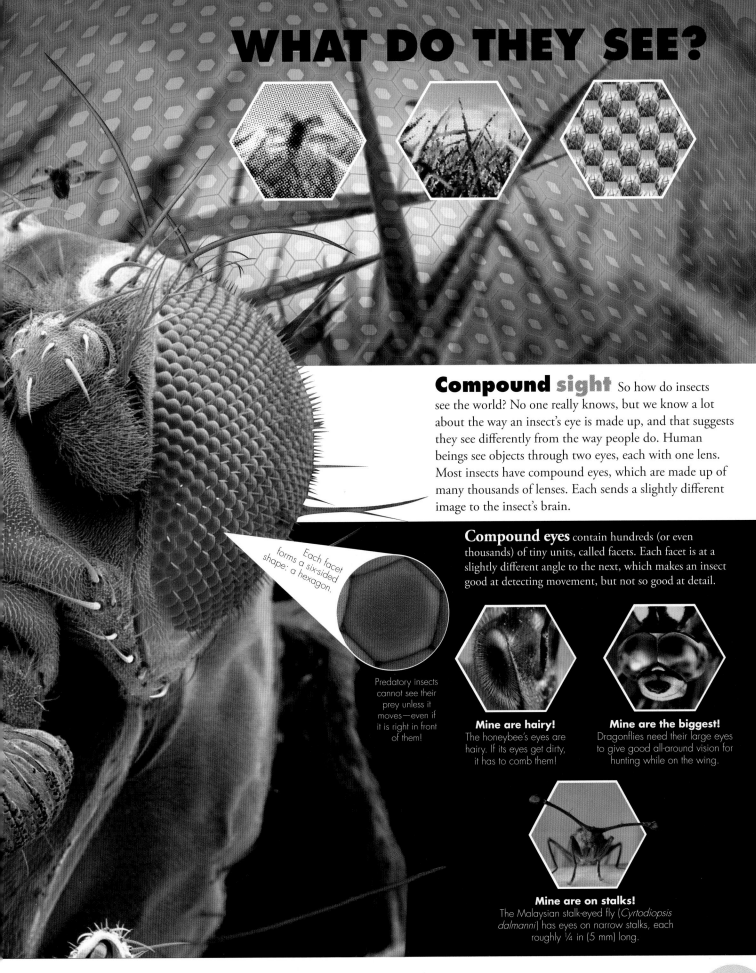

Compound sight
So how do insects see the world? No one really knows, but we know a lot about the way an insect's eye is made up, and that suggests they see differently from the way people do. Human beings see objects through two eyes, each with one lens. Most insects have compound eyes, which are made up of many thousands of lenses. Each sends a slightly different image to the insect's brain.

Each facet forms a six-sided shape: a hexagon.

Compound eyes
contain hundreds (or even thousands) of tiny units, called facets. Each facet is at a slightly different angle to the next, which makes an insect good at detecting movement, but not so good at detail.

Predatory insects cannot see their prey unless it moves—even if it is right in front of them!

Mine are hairy!
The honeybee's eyes are hairy. If its eyes get dirty, it has to comb them!

Mine are the biggest!
Dragonflies need their large eyes to give good all-around vision for hunting while on the wing.

Mine are on stalks!
The Malaysian stalk-eyed fly (*Cyrtodiopsis dalmanni*) has eyes on narrow stalks, each roughly ¼ in (5 mm) long.

FORELIMBS ACROSS THEIR EYES TO KEEP THEM CLEAN.

THE **HUNGER** BUG

Most people in the world will tuck into all sorts of **invertebrates** given the chance: perhaps you've tried lobster, shrimp, oysters, crayfish, crab, or a particular shellfish? They are all popular. Many people will happily **eat cooked insects and spiders** as well. There is actually little difference. The eating of insects even has a name: **ENTOMOPHAGY.**

BUGS FOR breakfast, lunch, *and dinner.* That one's **for** YOU. Save one for ME!

In **Bogotá, COLOMBIA,** moviegoers happily munch on roasted atta ant abdomens instead of popcorn.

What is eaten where?

Native Americans used to eat various insects, including caterpillars, but entomophagy is no longer widely practiced in North America (or in Europe).

In parts of **AFRICA**, termites are eaten with cornmeal porridge, adding valuable protein.

In **CHINA**, silkworm pupae (after the silk has been removed) are considered a delicacy.

In **JAPAN**, aquatic fly larvae are sautéed in sugar and soy sauce.

In **GHANA**, winged termites are fried, roasted, or crushed and made into bread.

Some outdoor markets in **THAILAND** sell fried insects by the bag.

In **SOUTH AFRICA**, a huge industry has been created around the mopane worm, a large edible caterpillar—it reaches about 4 in (10 cm) in length.

In **BALI**, you may find a dish consisting of dragonflies boiled in coconut milk and flavored with ginger and garlic.

In **NEW GUINEA** and **AUSTRALIA**, grubs have long been traditional "bush tucker." Another favorite bush food is live ants.

In **LATIN AMERICA**, people enjoy cicadas, fire-roasted tarantulas, red-legged grasshoppers, edible ants, and beetle larvae.

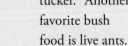

Why? PEOPLE EAT INSECTS AND SPIDERS because they like the taste. (Some people compare the taste of fried insects to that of crispy bacon.) They are also a good source of vitamins and minerals. And they are everywhere!

27

NOW YOU *see* ME…

... AND NOW YOU DON'T! INSECTS ARE MASTERS
OF DISGUISE. AFTER ALL, THEY DON'T WANT TO
BE EATEN. TAKE A LOOK AT JUST HOW GOOD
THEY ARE AT DISGUISING THEMSELVES.

TOP ROW: leaf bug, mantis, looper moth, stick insect, spiny bugs

MIDDLE ROW: ha   wk moth, katydid, katydid,   leaf insect

BOTTOM ROW: katydid, geometrid moths, orchid mantis,   thorn bugs, stick insect

90%
of all animal species are insects.

One-third of these are
beetles

There are more species of plant than there are species of beetle.

What makes a beetle a beetle?

A beetle is an insect, which means it has six legs and three body parts. Most beetles have two pairs of wings, but one pair is not used for flying—they are hard cases that protect the flying wings. There are more than 360,000 species of beetle described and many more yet to be discovered.

A person who studies beetles is called a coleopterist.

Beetles live everywhere on Earth, except in the oceans and around the freezing polar regions.

GLOW-IN-THE-DARK

IT TAKES 70,000 FIREFLIES TO MAKE AS MUCH LIGHT AS ONE LIGHTBULB

The twinkling lights that flit magically through woodlands on midsummer nights are FIREFLIES (2). They are not really flies but flying beetles, and their flashes are coded signals to mates. There are hundreds of firefly species, each with its own secret code of flashes. Some predatory fireflies even use trick codes to lure other species to their death. The glow comes from within a firefly's abdomen, where a chemical reaction releases light with near-perfect efficiency. A lightbulb wastes 90% of its energy as heat, but a firefly stays cold and releases almost 100% of the energy as light. GLOWWORMS (1) are the larvae of fireflies or the wingless females. The larvae can also produce light, not to attract mates but to warn predators that they taste nasty.

What other animals glow?

Besides fireflies, there are glowing gnats, glowing springtails, and many glowing sea animals. About 90% of deep-sea creatures produce light for one reason or another. Some, such as anglerfish, use light as a lure to catch prey. Others, including this glowing squid, spew out a cloud of glowing liquid to startle an enemy before making a quick getaway.

Do plants glow in the dark?

Organisms that produce light are described as "bioluminescent." There are no true bioluminescent plants, but some mushrooms produce light, perhaps to attract tiny gnats that help spread the mushrooms' spores. The eerie glow from these mushrooms is called "foxfire" and was used for portable lighting in the world's first submarines.

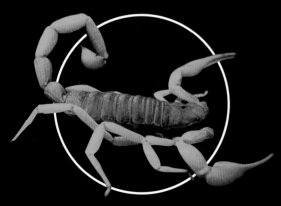

How do scorpions glow?

Scorpions can't produce light, but they do glow with a striking blue-green light when lit up with an ultraviolet lamp (a blacklight). The glow comes from fluorescent minerals in the skin, and nobody knows if it has a purpose. One advantage is that scorpions are very easy to find at night if you have a UV lamp!

Where does the light come from?

Fireflies, squids, and mushrooms all make light in a similar way: by making a substance called luciferin react with oxygen. Scientists have found the genes that control this chemical reaction and have figured out how to insert the genes into cancer cells to make them glow. The research could lead to important new discoveries about the way cancer spreads.

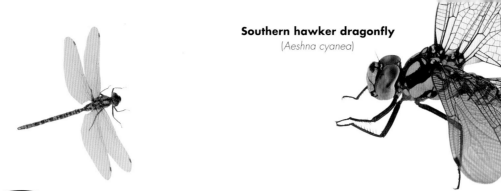

Southern hawker dragonfly
(Aeshna cyanea)

Growing *up*

The way insects grow up is nothing like the way humans do. Most insects go through a dramatic transformation as they turn into adults. Often, the change is so great that the adult looks totally different from the young insect. The changing process is called *metamorphosis*.

I'm a dragonfly nymph about to change into an adult. First I climb out of my pond and up a reed, where I cling on tightly...

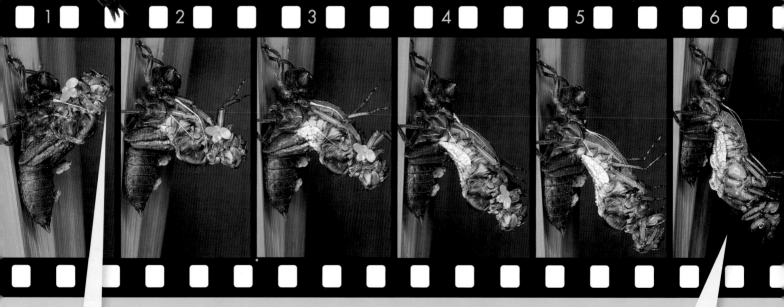

1　2　3　4　5　6

I split my skin for the final time and start to wriggle out.

My new skin has already formed, but at first it is very soft so I can squeeze out of the old skin. The new skin will harden after an hour or so.

Complete metamorphosis

Swallowtail butterfly

Pupa (chrysalis)

Larva (caterpillar)

Adult (butterfly)

In about 90% of insects, the young form is called a larva and looks nothing like the adult. It has no wings, no antennae, and no compound eyes. Caterpillars are the larvae of butterflies. A larva's job is simply to eat and grow. Then it forms a resting stage called a pupa. Inside the pupa, its body is broken down and rebuilt as an adult.

Simple growth

Silverfish

In a few insect species, metamorphosis doesn't happen. The youngsters are miniature replicas of the adult. They simply grow bigger, shedding their skin a few times to give room for growth.

Incomplete metamorphosis

Damselfly

Gills

Nymph

Damselflies, cockroaches, and various other insects grow up in stages. The youngsters, or nymphs, look like adults but have no wings. With each molt they get more like an adult, acquiring wings at the last stage. Dragonflies and damselflies live underwater as nymphs and change the most on their final molt.

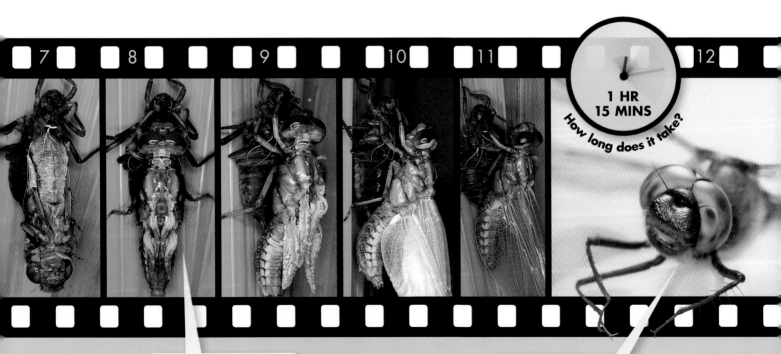

7 8 9 10 11 12

1 HR 15 MINS
How long does it take?

My wings are shriveled for now but will slowly expand. Then I'll fly for the first time.

Just over an hour after leaving the water, I fly away to begin my adult life.

Who's the daddy?

Match the parent to the child

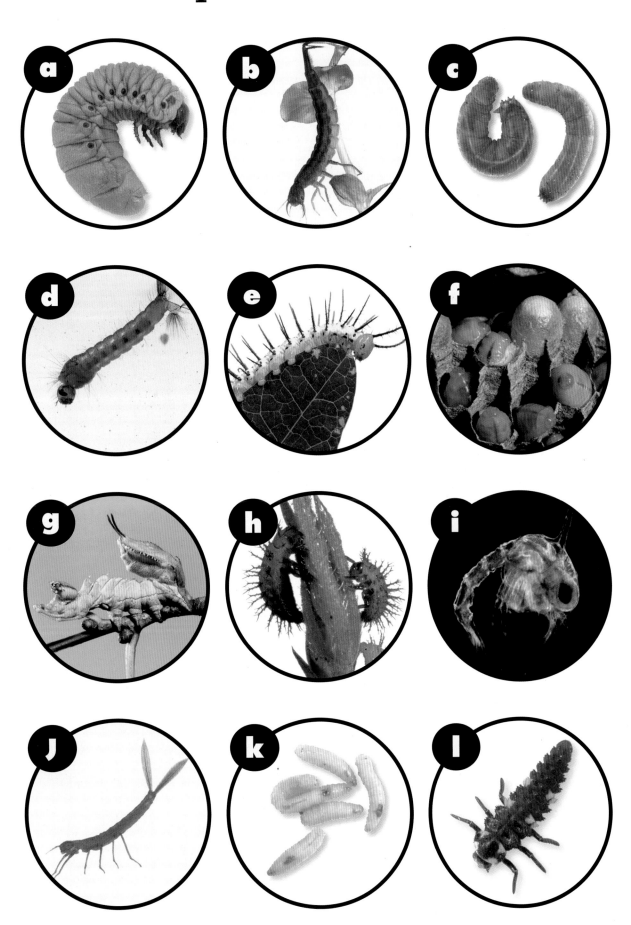

OUCH! You're stepping on my wing!

Different groups (broods) of cicada emerge nearly every year somewhere in North America, but the biggest and most spectacular is called "brood ten." It is next due in late spring 2021.

Yawn...

DAY 1

I'm a young cicada—a "nymph." I live underground and feed on the root of a plant. I spend 17 years here, in the dark, without moving. It's kind of boring...

After 17 years I've nearly grown up and it's time to escape from my underground hiding place. In the middle of the night, I dig an escape tunnel and crawl out into the open. Millions of young cicadas all come out at the same time. We all clamber up trees and plants to find a safe place for an amazing transformation...

It's time to molt. I shed my skin and crawl out with my adult body.

GET OUT OF MY WAY!

DAY 5

There are millions of us in the forest now. Predators will catch a lot of us, but there are far too many for the predators to eat. Most of us will survive.

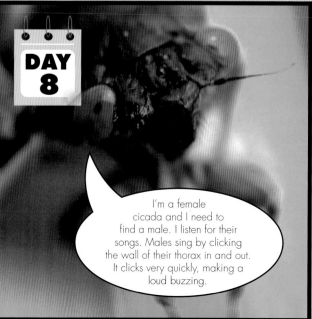

DAY 8

I'm a female cicada and I need to find a male. I listen for their songs. Males sing by clicking the wall of their thorax in and out. It clicks very quickly, making a loud buzzing.

DAY 10

ONCE IN A BLUE MOON

The amazing periodical cicada spends precisely 13 or 17 years of its life hidden underground as a youngster. Then it crawls out in the dead of night to grow up and lead its short adult life. Every 13 or 17 years, vast numbers of cicadas emerge at once in the forests of North America. They cover the trees and fill the air with sound, creating one of the wonders of the natural world.

Orange sulphur
(*Colias eurytheme*)

Small copper
(*Lycaena phlaeas*)

Butterfly

Tiger swallowtail
(*Papilio glaucus*)

Australian regent skipper
(*Euschemon rafflesia*)

Small white
(*Pieris rapae*)

Day flight
Most butterflies fly during the day, but some fly at dusk. None fly at night. The sun warms their flight muscles.

Antennae
Most butterflies have thin antennae. All have a small, rounded club at the tip.

Body
Butterflies tend to have smooth, thin bodies.

Feeding
Butterflies use a proboscis (which is sort of like a coiled drinking straw) to feed on nectar.

At rest
Most butterflies rest with their wings upright and together.

Pupa
A butterfly pupa, also called a chrysalis, has a protective hard shell and often hangs from a leaf.

Common blue
(*Polyommatus icarus*)

Small postman
(*Heliconius erato*)

Camberwell beauty
(*Nymphalis antiopa*)

Common green birdwing
(*Ornithoptera priamus*)

Orange tip butterfly
(*Anthocharis cardamines*)

Queen Alexandra's birdwing
(*Ornithoptera alexandrae*)

Monarch butterfly
(*Danaus plexippus*)

Blue morpho
(*Morpho menelaus*)

Both butterflies and moths belong to the same insect group: the Lepidoptera,

or Moth?

Butterflies evolved from moths, and they share many features. But here are some signs to help you spot the difference...

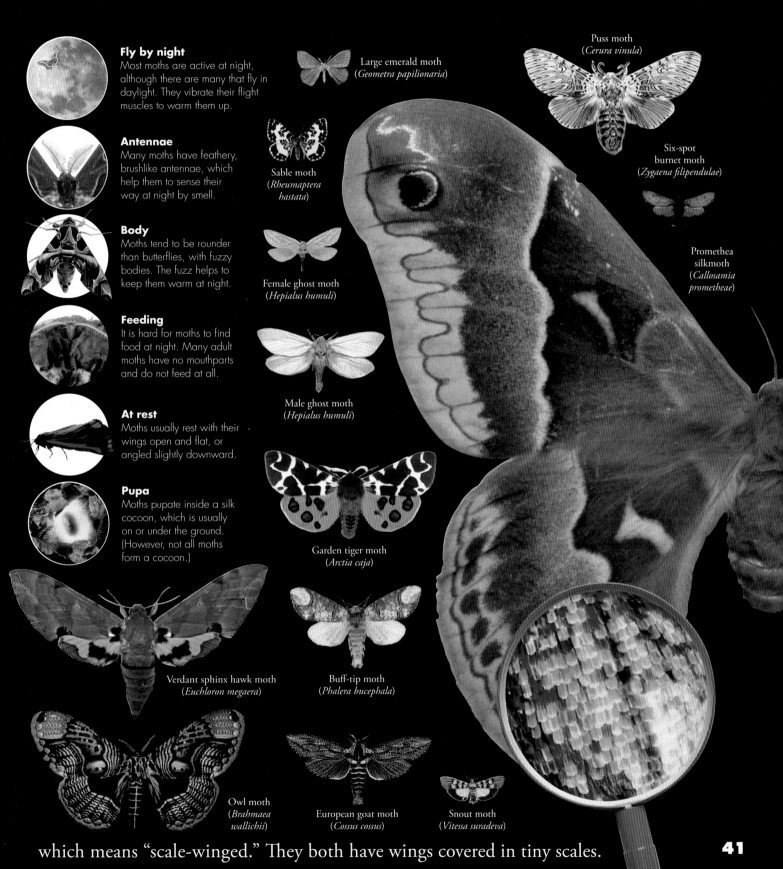

Fly by night
Most moths are active at night, although there are many that fly in daylight. They vibrate their flight muscles to warm them up.

Antennae
Many moths have feathery, brushlike antennae, which help them to sense their way at night by smell.

Body
Moths tend to be rounder than butterflies, with fuzzy bodies. The fuzz helps to keep them warm at night.

Feeding
It is hard for moths to find food at night. Many adult moths have no mouthparts and do not feed at all.

At rest
Moths usually rest with their wings open and flat, or angled slightly downward.

Pupa
Moths pupate inside a silk cocoon, which is usually on or under the ground. (However, not all moths form a cocoon.)

Large emerald moth
(*Geometra papilionaria*)

Sable moth
(*Rheumaptera hastata*)

Female ghost moth
(*Hepialus humuli*)

Male ghost moth
(*Hepialus humuli*)

Garden tiger moth
(*Arctia caja*)

Verdant sphinx hawk moth
(*Euchloron megaera*)

Buff-tip moth
(*Phalera bucephala*)

Owl moth
(*Brahmaea wallichii*)

European goat moth
(*Cossus cossus*)

Snout moth
(*Vitessa suradeva*)

Puss moth
(*Cerura vinula*)

Six-spot burnet moth
(*Zygaena filipendulae*)

Promethea silkmoth
(*Callosamia prometheae*)

which means "scale-winged." They both have wings covered in tiny scales.

41

MEET THE
MONARCHS

The **extraordinary** story of the monarch butterfly.

For such a small creature, the colorful monarch butterfly undergoes a remarkable journey. As the first fall leaves start to fall, thousands of these butterflies gather in southern *Canada* and other parts of *North America* to migrate south. Some will travel almost 3,000 miles (4,800 km), heading for the warmer climates of *California* and *Mexico*.

Caterpillar

Chrysalis

Butterfly

ONE OF SEVERAL
FLIGHT PATHS OF THE
MONARCH BUTTERFLY IN
NORTH AMERICA

Life **patterns**

1 **MARCH–APRIL:** The first generation of monarchs is born. They undergo full metamorphosis, from egg to caterpillar to chrysalis to adult butterfly. They mate, lay eggs, and then die.

2 **MAY–JUNE:** The second generation is born. Their lives follow the pattern of the first generation.

3 **JULY–AUGUST:** The third generation is born, undergoes metamorphosis, and dies.

4 **SEPTEMBER–NOVEMBER:** The fourth generation does not die so soon. They MIGRATE south on an incredibly long journey and then hibernate in a winter roost for five to seven months in Mexico or southern California. They awaken and begin mating in February and March of the NEXT SPRING, and then start the long journey north, and lay their eggs. They finally die. Young monarchs find their way back to the breeding grounds of the first generation on instinct; older butterflies don't show them the way!

At one sanctuary in Mexico, near Angangueo, it is estimated that every winter some 100 million monarch butterflies arrive from North America. The air is filled with the sound of their fluttering wings.

Monarchs are poisonous and they taste awful. Predators soon learn to avoid them.

It takes **four** generations to make this *incredible* journey. The *fourth* generation does **MOST** of the work.

A Silkworm's Story

The first thing you need to know is that I am not a worm. I am the caterpillar of a Chinese moth, and the single thread I spin for my cocoon has been harvested by people to use as silk for at least 4,000 years.

Females cannot fly, while males cannot fly very well. So a male needs a female to be close by, or he will not find her. The adult males die soon after mating. The females die after laying eggs.

My species has never lived in the wild. In fact, we are entirely dependent on human beings for reproduction. I'm a male, and my feathery antennae help me to pick up the scent of a female.

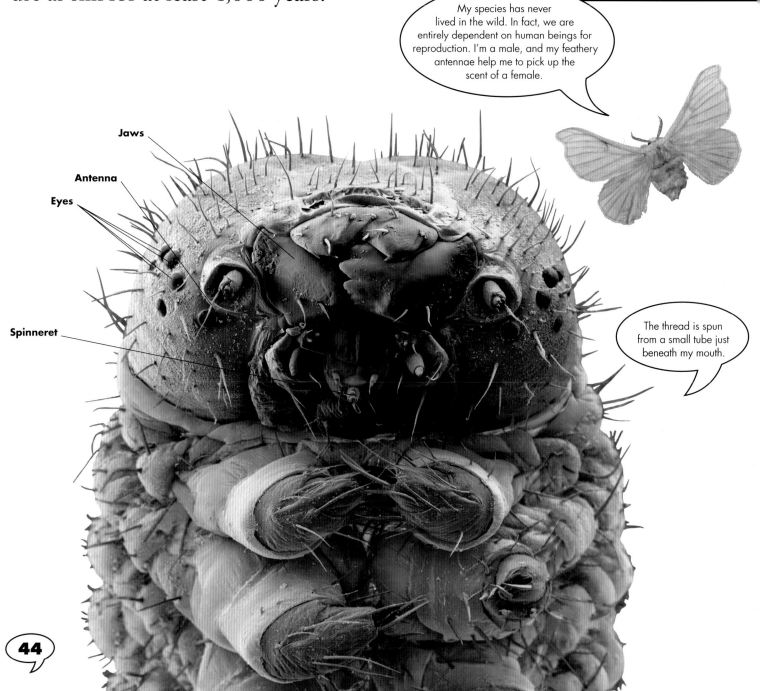

Jaws

Antenna

Eyes

Spinneret

The thread is spun from a small tube just beneath my mouth.

LOCUST PLAGUE

A locust *attack* can be **devastating.**

JUST FOLLOWING THE CROWD...

Desert locusts normally lead solitary lives, but they can undergo an amazing change. If enough food grows, lots of locusts are able to hatch. The overcrowding makes them completely change the way they look: they become shorter and turn a different color.

African desert locust *(Schistocerca gregaria)*

WILL I STAY A LONELY LOCUST OR BECOME A PARTY ANIMAL?

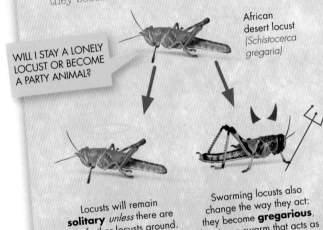

Locusts will remain **solitary** *unless* there are lots of other locusts around. They stay green and cause relatively little damage.

Swarming locusts also change the way they act: they become **gregarious**, forming a swarm that acts as one unit, *devastating* crops.

WANTED

FROM THE INFAMOUS LOCUST GANG—HE'S **DESTRUCTIVE!**

Huge REWARD

...if **you** can find a means of stopping the desert locust from wreaking **havoc**.

I just need to eat. What's the problem?

What's the solution?

Unfortunately, once the **African desert locust** descends, there is nothing a farmer can do but watch as crops are hungrily devoured. Scientists are trying to help by predicting where a swarm may break out, but the swarms are so big, they quickly take control.

A cloud appears

Locust swarms first appear as a dark cloud on the horizon. They can travel 80 miles (130 km) a day, so when they settle, they are hungry! They will strip a field in minutes, leaving it bare, and they are widespread. Swarms have been reported in at least 60 of the world's countries.

Above: Locust eating
Right: Swarm of locusts on crops

What's for lunch?

Locusts have taste and touch sensors all over their bodies. They can quickly assess whether or not a crop is good to eat.

85¢

October 10, 1996

The International Paper

Plague returns

Farmers in large parts of Eastern Africa have been reporting increasing numbers of locust swarms. These insects have been feared by farmers in many parts of Africa and Asia for thousands of years—a locust can eat its own weight in a day. A third of a square mile (1 sq km) may contain 80 million of the creatures, while a swarm can cover hundreds of miles. During one plague in Somalia, the locusts devoured enough food to feed 400,000 people for a whole year.

A locust swarm passes over.

Who's for dinner?

What's the most *disgusting* substance you can think of? Whatever it is, it's delicious to arthropods. Arthropods can eat and digest nearly every kind of organic substance on our planet.

All kinds of arthropods dine on live humans. The **head louse** clambers through your hair and snacks on blood by biting your skin. **Mosquitos** land for one bite and fly away full of blood. Scabies mites dig tunnels inside your skin and make you itch. Botfly maggots burrow into muscles and sit there for weeks, eating your flesh.

The poor **silkmoth** doesn't eat anything during its whole adult life. It can't—it doesn't have a working mouth. It lives for only a few days and then dies of starvation and thirst.

Fruit flies like the taste of rotting fruit—the natural source of alcohol. Just like humans, they get drunk and pass out if they have too much. But they never get addicted.

Not many animals can digest wood, but **termites** can. If they get into your house, they can eat their way through floorboards and beams until the whole building collapses.

Silverfish are fond of books, but rather than reading them they eat the glue that holds the pages together. Failing that, they eat the pages themselves. They aren't greedy—they survive on tiny amounts and can live for a year without eating anything.

Clothes moths eat fabrics made of animal hairs. Wool socks, fur coats, and carpets are all ideal. In the wild, these moths feed on the pelts of dead animals.

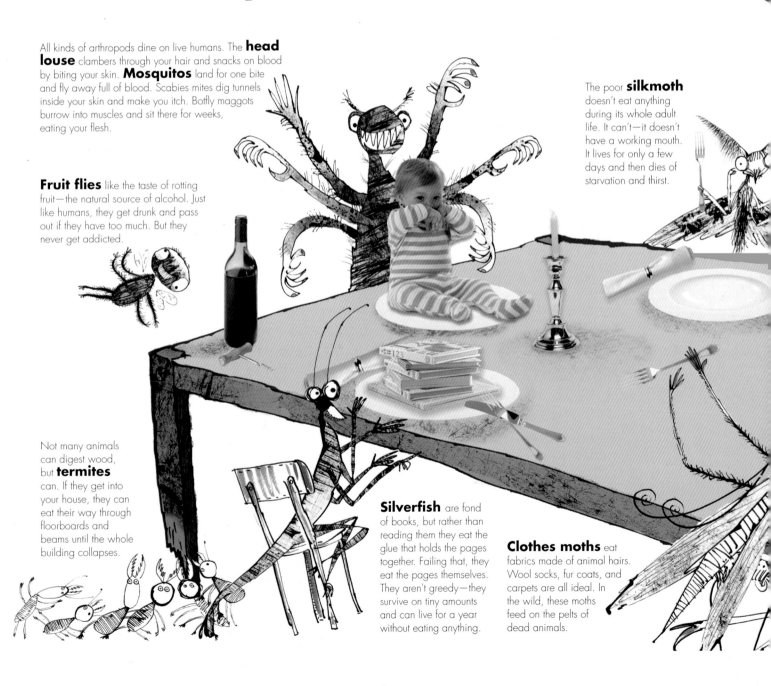

Check out the menu...

THE MENU

1. One sumptuously smelly sock
2. A lovely, sweet, fleshy baby
3. A delectable dollop of dung
4. A crunchy coil of cardboard
5. Your very own mother
6. A tower of tasty tomes
7. Nothing at all, not a crumb!

A stinking ball of excrement is the perfect meal for a **dung beetle**. Dung beetle larvae chew their way through dung from the inside, but adults prefer to squeeze fresh dollops and suck out the delicious juices.

Australian social spiders start life by eating their mother. Having fattened herself up deliberately, the mother lets her newly hatched babies suck her blood. When she's too weak to move, they attack her with venomous bites and devour her body completely.

The **jewel wasp** (below) stings a cockroach in the brain to stop it from running around. Then the wasp lays an egg on the cockroach. The egg hatches and the larva burrows into the cockroach and eats it.

I LOVE MUM

Cockroaches will dig into almost any kind of garbage, from cardboard and soap to stale dog food and fingernail clippings. Yum!

All work and no play

Leaf-cutter ants live in enormous colonies. The colonies work because each member has a particular job to do. It's hard and they stick to it day and night. So what do they do? They are farmers.

I am a **leaf cutter**. I fetch and carry leaves back to the nest. I cut them to size if necessary.

Some of us make sure the pathways to and from the nest are kept free of debris. You could call me a **street sweeper**.

How do we know where to go to find the best leaves? We leave a scent trail.

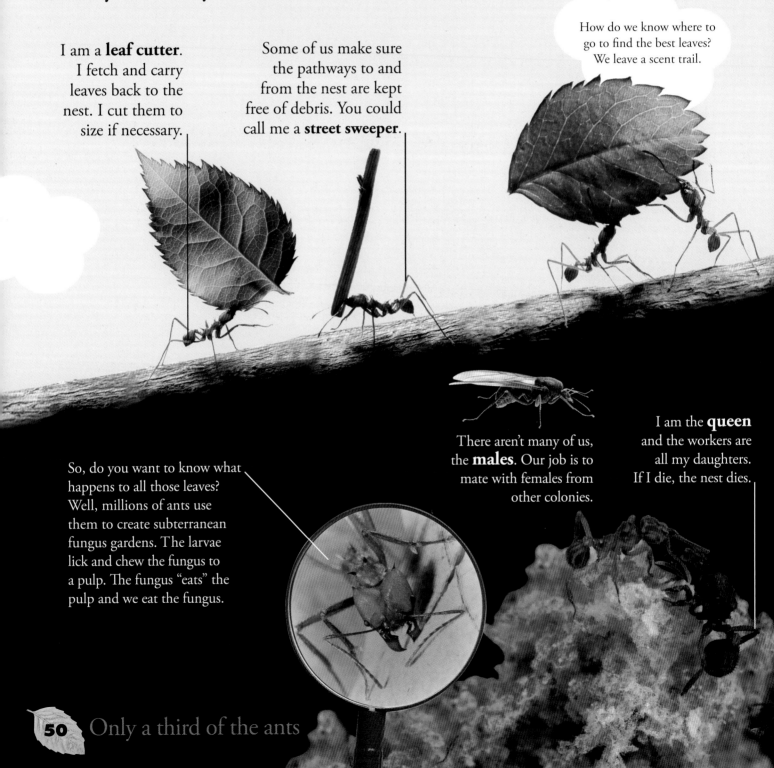

There aren't many of us, the **males**. Our job is to mate with females from other colonies.

I am the **queen** and the workers are all my daughters. If I die, the nest dies.

So, do you want to know what happens to all those leaves? Well, millions of ants use them to create subterranean fungus gardens. The larvae lick and chew the fungus to a pulp. The fungus "eats" the pulp and we eat the fungus.

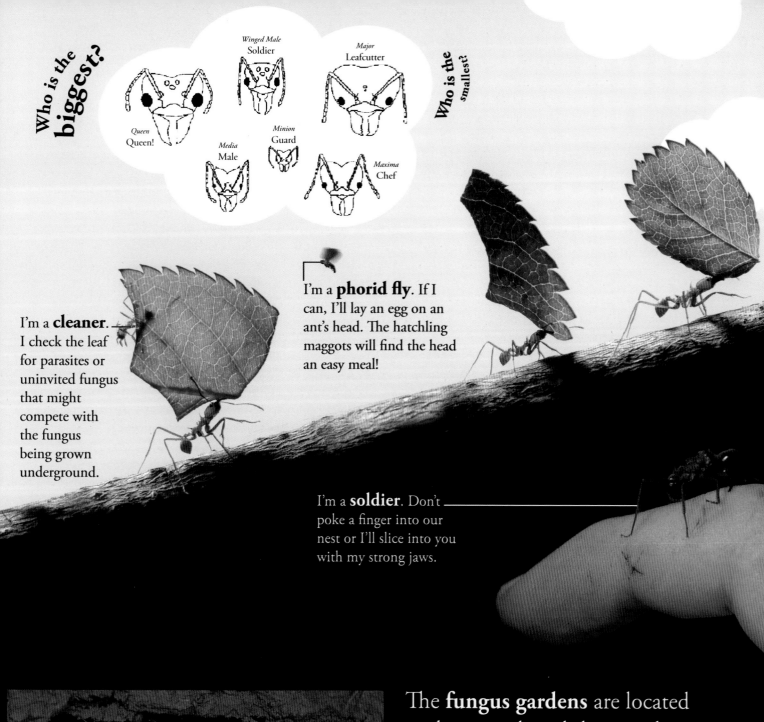

Who is the **biggest?**

Queen
Queen!

Winged Male
Soldier

Media
Male

Minion
Guard

Major
Leafcutter

Maxima
Chef

Who is the **smallest?**

I'm a **cleaner**. I check the leaf for parasites or uninvited fungus that might compete with the fungus being grown underground.

I'm a **phorid fly**. If I can, I'll lay an egg on an ant's head. The hatchling maggots will find the head an easy meal!

I'm a **soldier**. Don't poke a finger into our nest or I'll slice into you with my strong jaws.

The **fungus gardens** are located underground, and they can be huge! That's because to cultivate enough fungus, the ants must collect massive quantities of leaves, bit by tiny bit. The chambers are stacked above each other, sometimes to a depth of 20 feet (6 meters).

in a nest come out to collect leaves. The others work away in darkness

51

ARMY ANTS

NEWS FLASH > THEY'RE COMING!

You turn at a rustle on the forest floor. Looking closely, you notice that a surprisingly large number of small insects are scrambling to escape. The rustle grows louder, now accompanied by a distinct hissing, and you begin to notice ants. Thousands of ants. These are killers, and they will overcome and eat whatever lies in their path, cutting it apart and taking it back to their nest. They can quickly subdue centipedes, scorpions, tarantulas, and vertebrates, such as lizards and frogs.

The marching column is made up of female ants, none of whom can lay eggs. They are the workers and there may be 20 million of them. There are very few males.

I'm a winged male driver ant. Look at my sausage-shaped abdomen.

WINGED MALE
ANT NO. 240300
NICKNAME:
SAUSAGE FLY

Large prey such as a scorpion is no obstacle to army ants. A single ant may discover it, and will then release chemicals to draw other ants toward it. The scorpion will soon be buried under a mass of ants.

...1,000s of **army ants.**

Army ants are social insects, working together to form colonies that are highly efficient at tasks such as rearing young and subduing prey. They frequently move from place to place, otherwise they would run out of food. They can even build living bridges to cross obstacles on the forest floor.

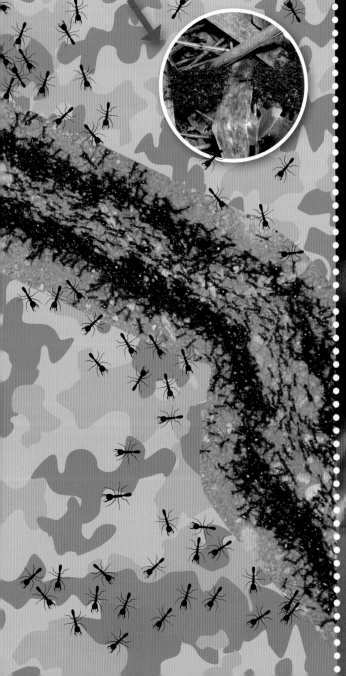

So who are the killers?

There are two main types of ant that forage in armies: the army ants of North, South, and Central America, and the driver ants of Africa. There are some differences. Army ants have a powerful sting. Driver ants use sharp mandibles (jaws) to slice away at their victims. Army ants can't kill large vertebrates, but driver ants can—they may overpower a chicken, or an injured pig. Most large creatures can move out of the way, but arthropods can't move quickly enough. In Africa, driver ants have been known to raid villages, which can be helpful. The inhabitants simply move out while the ants clean out the cockroaches and mice that may have seen it as a safe home. All army ants form temporary homes, called bivouacs, constructing them by hooking themselves together.

I protect the worker ants with my powerful jaws. Above is our home, a bivouac of living ants.

Who is in the hive?

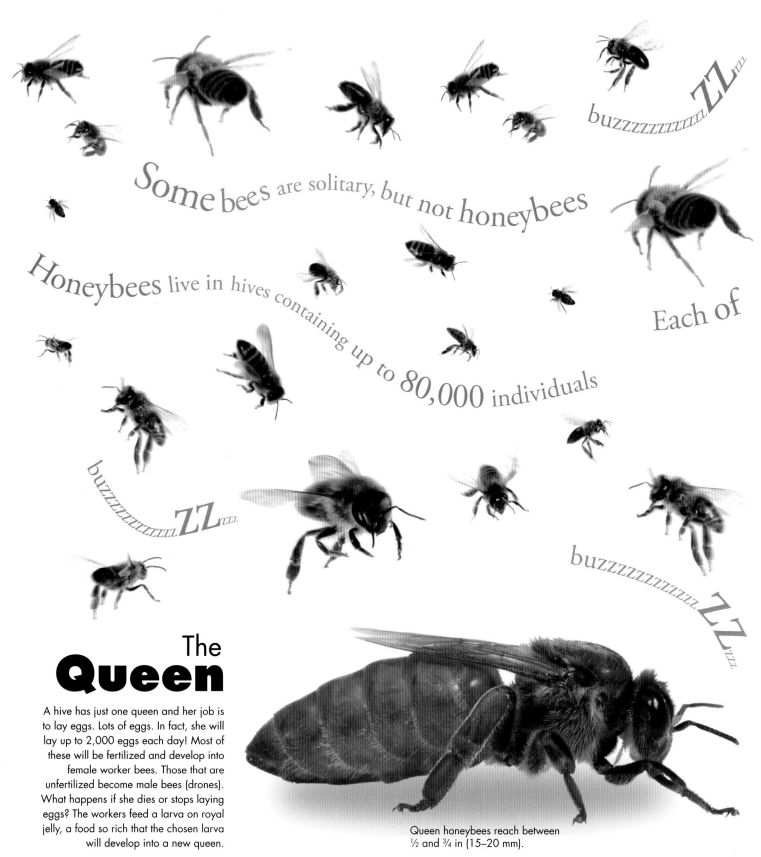

Some bees are solitary, but not honeybees

buzzzzzzzzzzzzz ZZ zzz

Honeybees live in hives containing up to 80,000 individuals

Each of

buzzzzzzzzzzzz ZZ zzz

buzzzzzzzzzzzzz ZZ zzz

The Queen

A hive has just one queen and her job is to lay eggs. Lots of eggs. In fact, she will lay up to 2,000 eggs each day! Most of these will be fertilized and develop into female worker bees. Those that are unfertilized become male bees (drones). What happens if she dies or stops laying eggs? The workers feed a larva on royal jelly, a food so rich that the chosen larva will develop into a new queen.

Queen honeybees reach between ½ and ¾ in (15–20 mm).

these bees has a specific job to do

buzzzzzzzzzzzzzzzZZ

buzzzzzzzzzzzzzzz

The
Worker

Most of the bees in a hive are female workers. From their first appearance to their last breath, they work, work, and work. For the first 12 days, they clean the cells that store honey, nurse the larvae, and tend to the queen. Those between 12 and 20 days old build and repair cells, collect and store the nectar and pollen brought into the hive, and act as guards, checking the identity of returning workers. After 20 days, workers begin to forage, leaving the hive to return laden with nectar and pollen.

Workers reach
up to ½ in (15 mm)
in length.

The
Drone

A hive contains between 300 and 3,000 drones (male bees), but only in the summer months. In the fall the drones are thrown out because they are not needed. In the summer, it's a different story: male bees are kept on standby for mating with queens in other hives. They are well looked after, but it's not all easy—if they do mate, they die. Unlike the workers, the drone does not have a stinger.

Drones reach
about ¾ in (18 mm).

How did
this

There are lots of different flavored honeys. Flavor depends on the flowers the bees visited when collecting the nectar.

Beeswax crayons last longer than other crayons and the colors can be mixed. Blue and yellow *will* make green.

Beeswax is a perfect material for candle-making. Beeswax candles smell of honey—and they don't drip.

Light **honey**

Clear **honey**

Comb **honey**

Dark **honey**

Spun **honey**

produce
this honey?

In addition to so many other things that we find useful?

Honeybees are incredibly useful to us. We not only steal their honey, but we also use beeswax for an almost endless list of items, from crayons and creams to polishes and soaps. Of course, bees don't actually make the honey or wax for human use. Honey is a product of nectar, which is collected by worker bees from flowers and thickened in the hive for use as bee food. Wax is produced by young bees when they are building and repairing their hive. Each bee will produce a tiny flake of wax and some 500,000 of these go into every 1 lb (0.5 kg) of beeswax. The bees use the flakes to shape honeycomb cells into which the eggs are laid. Humans find hundreds of additional uses for the wax.

56

In its lifetime, each honeybee will probably produce just 1 teaspoon of honey.

Skyscraper

How can this tiny insect build an **air-conditioned**, **multiroomed** tower with walls as hard as **concrete**?

For a start, he needs a lot of friends, and it can still take up to 50 years to complete. Yet for their size, termites build the largest structures of any living creature! Termites live in huge colonies. Their mounds are built to help them survive the hot and dry climates they inhabit and to protect them from predators. Different types of termite build mounds of different shapes and sizes.

Compass termite mounds are found in northern Australia. They are always orientated a certain way.

This umbrella mound was built by African termites to withstand heavy rain.

The London landmark known as the Gherkin is built to take advantage of natural air-conditioning, drawing in air like a termite mound.

Termite queens can grow to more than 6 in (15 cm)!

A feat of engineering

Outside, the temperature may reach 104°F (40°C), but inside, a termite mound maintains a constant, comfortable temperature. It's a perfect environment for food pantries, gardens, and, of course, nurseries for all those baby termites. Dedicated chambers for these purposes are placed at specific points inside the mound, and they usually have arched ceilings (for strength). There's even a royal chamber for the king and queen. A clever system of tunnels and chimneys ensures that air flows around the nest, and the mound even has foundations so it doesn't collapse, just like a brick-built house. And all this is achieved without teams of architects and engineers poring over plans and drawings.

Termites are just under ½ in (1 cm) in length, but they can build mounds that are taller than 20 ft (6 m).

This Australian cathedral mound may be around 100 years old.

I'm an average height, but just look at how **BIG** this tower is!

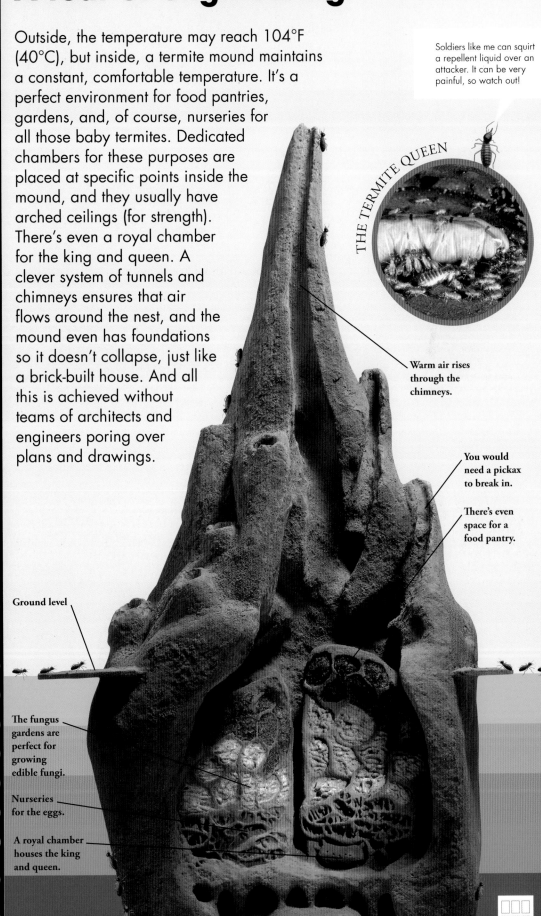

Soldiers like me can squirt a repellent liquid over an attacker. It can be very painful, so watch out!

THE TERMITE QUEEN

Warm air rises through the chimneys.

You would need a pickax to break in.

There's even space for a food pantry.

Ground level

The fungus gardens are perfect for growing edible fungi.

Nurseries for the eggs.

A royal chamber houses the king and queen.

WHOO-whoo
SPOT *the* FAKE

The caterpillar of a Costa Rican hawkmoth can inflate its body to imitate the head of a venomous viper. Glaring eyespots complete the disguise.

Viceroy (top) and monarch (bottom) butterflies mimic each other. Both species are foul tasting to birds, and the similar patterns reinforce the message.

Bushy antennae and outspread wings are clues that the top "bee" here is really just a harmless moth. The disguise scares off birds that have learned to avoid bees.

A cunning way to defend yourself from attack is to pretend to be something nasty. All the creatures on the top row here are mimicking the dangerous animals below. The disguises aren't perfect, but they are good enough to fool a predator for the few seconds it takes to make a getaway.

Look closely at the wingtips of the atlas moth. Some people think they resemble the head of a deadly cobra poised to spit out venom.

Count the legs on the top "ant." It's actually a jumping spider disguised as an ant so it can lurk near the ants' colony for protection.

The hoverfly's wasplike stripes are there to fool birds, but even humans are sometimes afraid of these harmless insects.

Leg (1 of 8)

Giant house spider

Spiders have small, armlike pedipalps that are used used to transfer sperm during mating, as well as to handle food.

Opisthosoma (rear segment)

Prosoma (front segment)

Chelicerae (contain fangs)

Arachnophobia

Scared of spiders? Arachnids make up the second biggest branch of the arthropod family tree after insects. They aren't just spiders. Scorpions belong to this class of arthropod, as do ticks and mites, which are the most common arachnid. All these creatures have certain key things in common. They are best known for having eight legs, but they also have four other appendages (called chelicerae and pedipalps) that flank the mouth and work as fangs, feelers, or claws. Unlike insects, arachnids don't have compound eyes or antennae, and their bodies have only two main segments. Many are flesh-eaters, and most are ruthlessly efficient killing machines.

Imperial scorpion

Scorpions have huge pedipalps that are used as claws for catching food.

Harvestman
Often mistaken for a spider, the harvestman (daddy longlegs) belongs to a separate branch of the arachnid family tree. Unlike a spider, it has no silk glands or venom glands. Its amazingly long legs make it a very good climber, and they twitch if snapped off, perhaps to distract predators.

Tailless whip scorpion
This peculiar arachnid walks sideways on six of its legs while using its extraordinarily long front legs (called whips) to feel around for prey. Once found, prey is grasped in huge, folding claws and ripped apart.

Scorpion
Large claws and sting-tipped tails make scorpions unmistakeable. The most ancient of arachnids, they live only in hot countries and hunt by night. As a rule of thumb, the more menacing a scorpion looks, the less dangerous it is. The deadliest kinds are small, with spindly pincers but fat tails packed with venom.

House spider
The house spider is often found trapped in a bathtub after falling from the ceiling. A member of the funnel-web family, it builds a messy, sheetlike web with a funnel-shaped den. Other members of this family are deadly (see page 71), but the house spider's bite isn't dangerous or particularly painful.

Mite

Dust mite

Mites are found in vast numbers everywhere. A bed can contain two million dust mites, which eat dead human skin. Most mites are smaller than periods, so we seldom see them.

actual size

Tick

Ticks are bloodsucking parasites. They lurk in forests and meadows waiting for animals to brush past and pick them up. Then they stab their harpoon-shaped mouth into the skin and swell up like balloons as they fill with blood.

After feeding

Before feeding

Garden spider

Members of the orb spider family, such as this garden spider, trap prey in circular webs made from spirals of silk. Prey are killed by a venomous bite and sucked dry.

Trapdoor spider

Rather than trapping prey in a web, trapdoor spiders hide in a burrow with a camouflaged trapdoor and leap out when they feel prey walking on top.

Red-kneed tarantula

Huntsman spider

Agile and quick-footed, this spider hunts on foot. It can sprint up walls and across ceilings, and can even dart sideways like a crab. If you pick one up it is likely to cling on and may bite in self-defense.

Tarantula

With legspans of up to 12 in (30 cm) and fangs up to 1 in (2.5 cm) long, tarantulas are the giants of the spider world and can kill birds, bats, and mice. In captivity they can live for 30 years.

Jumping spider

Bulbous eyes give the tiny jumping spiders the best vision in the spider world. Instead of spinning webs they hunt on foot, carefully sneaking up on victims when they aren't looking.

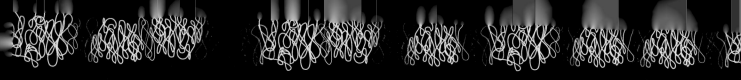

This magnified length of spider's silk shows just why it stretches so well.

The same silk s t r e t c h e d by five times its length.

The silk has been **s t r e t c h e d** 20 times its original length.

A spider's web is a feat of **engineering**,

and a spiral **orb web** is built in a particular way and usually at night. It takes the spider about ONE HOUR to build. Easily damaged by wind and rain, a spider may have to **repair** its web two or three times a day.

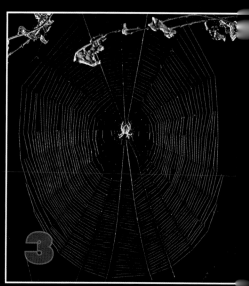

A spider has spun and attached draglines to anchor its new web. These radiate from a central point. It now begins to work around the center.

As the spider works, the threads that touch will stick together, strengthening the web. A web called a spiral orb is beginning to emerge.

The spider now waits at the center of the finished web. It will respond rapidly to any vibrations, since these are caused when an insect is caught.

Web-spinning spiders are born with the skill;
no spider is taught how to make a web. Scientists
discovered this by isolating baby spiders.

Different **types** of **spider** build different types of **web**.

Funnel

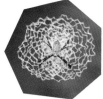

Spiral

Tangle

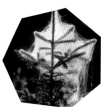

Sheet

Funnel webs
These webs are often built in hidden corners; in cracks in fences or holes in a tree. The spider retreats into the funnel and waits for an insect to get caught before pouncing.

Orb webs
These flat, spiral webs are perhaps the most common of all spider webs. The spider lays draglines, and then completes the web by working around and around and around.

Tangle webs
These are amazing webs, and they can cover the top of a shrub. The web is a confusion of tangled threads, from which an unfortunate insect has no escape.

Sheet webs
These distinctive webs are so named because the central tangle is a horizontal sheet. Crossed threads above and below the sheet knock flying insects into the sheet.

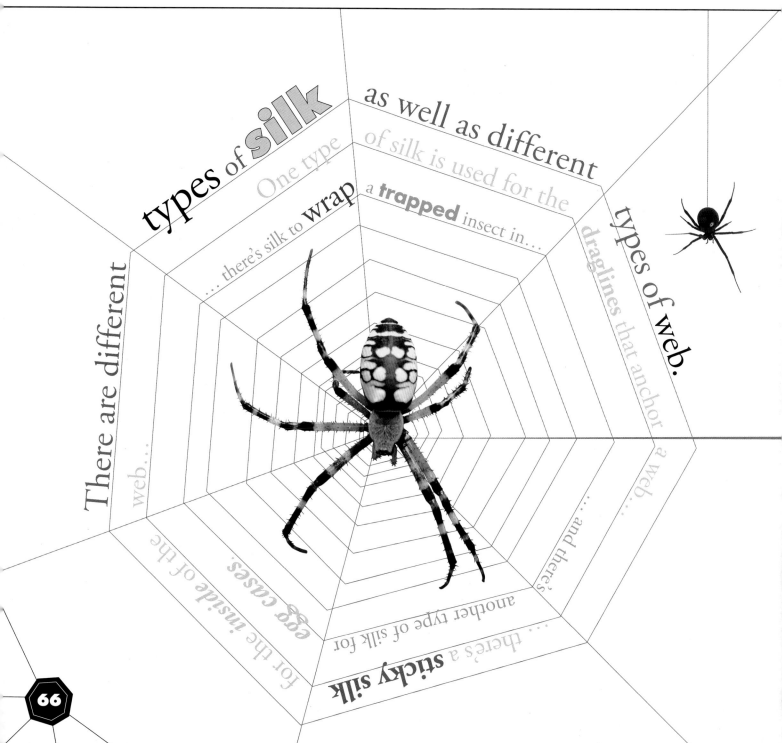

There are different types of **silk** as well as different types of web.

One type... there's silk to **wrap** a **trapped** insect in... of silk is used for the draglines that anchor a web... and there's another type of silk for the inside of the egg cases. ...there's a **sticky silk** web...

web**masters**

There is more to a spider's web than meets the eye—not only is it strong, it's s-t-r-e-t-c-h-y as well—which makes it ideal for catching insects. And not weight for weight, the silk strands are some five times stronger than steel.

Draglines are produced when a spider starts a web, to anchor it securely.

People have used (and still use) spider silk for all kinds of things, including fishing lures, lines, and netting. The largest and strongest spider web of all is built by the Darwin's bark spider of Madagascar. This spider's web can span 25 m (82ft) wide, the length of three African bush elephants. Its silk is 10 times stronger than the super-strong artificial material Kevlar.

When a web needs to be **repaired** the spider will eat the silk and start again.

Stronger than steel

Scientists estimate that if dragline silk (the silk a spider dangles on) could be reproduced with the diameter of a pencil, it would be strong enough to stop a large jet plane in flight.

A spider that is fed coffee will make irregular webs.

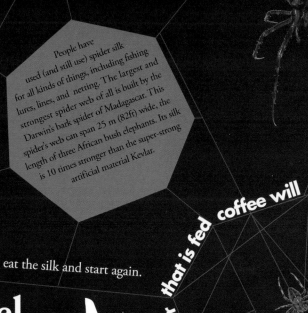

Wide-spaced thread lines.

Wolf spider

NOT all spiders build webs

Ground spiders don't, and crab spiders don't. Instead, they hide in leaves and flowers waiting to pounce. Wolf spiders do this, choosing to hunt at night.

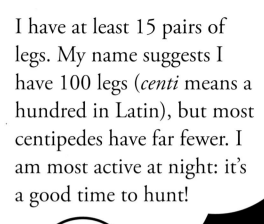

I have at least 15 pairs of legs. My name suggests I have 100 legs (*centi* means a hundred in Latin), but most centipedes have far fewer. I am most active at night: it's a good time to hunt!

Centipede

Centipedes are **carnivores** that feed on small invertebrates.

Centipedes **run** away if attacked.

Centipedes have **one pair** of legs per segment.

Centipedes are **fast** runners.

Centipedes generally have **flattened** bodies.

For its size, a centipede is faster than a cheetah.

Many centipedes have venomous claws located under their heads that are used to kill their prey.

or Millipede?

Feeling threatened, a pill millipede rolls into a tight ball.

Most millipedes are **vegetarians**. They feed on decaying vegetation.

Millipedes **roll** into a **ball** if attacked.

Millipedes have **two pairs** of legs per segment.

Millipedes are **slow**-moving.

Millipedes generally have **rounded** bodies.

Some millipedes produce a bad smell when they sense a threat.

My name suggests I have 1,000 legs, but no millipede has 1,000 legs; most have around 60, although some have 750. There are a lot more species of millipede than centipede. You'll usually find me burrowing through leaf litter, especially in damp conditions.

DANGER!

Suicide mission

Honeybees kill more people than any other venomous animal. African honeybees are the deadliest. If you step too close to their nest, guard bees release an alarm scent that makes the colony attack as a swarm. They chase relentlessly, delivering hundreds of stings. Bees only die when they attack thick-skinned targets like humans. When routinely attacking in defense of hive, they can sting again and again.

Beetle bomb

The bombardier beetle stores explosive chemicals inside two chambers in its abdomen. If you upset this beetle, it will force the two chemicals together so they react and explode. Boiling, caustic chemicals blast out through a swiveling nozzle that the beetle can aim. If the spray hits a small animal in the face, it can blind or kill it.

All these arthropods use **chemical weapons** to **defend** themselves.

Chemical warfare

Bristly hairs

In addition to using their venomous fangs for defense, tarantulas can flick a barrage of toxic hairs at attackers. Special urticating hairs grow on the abdomen and are flicked off with the legs. The hairs lodge in skin and release chemicals that cause a rash. If they get in your eyes, they can cause excruciating pain.

Stink bomb

Stink bugs have special glands in the thorax that secrete a foul-smelling liquid when the bugs are handled. If you hold one in cupped hands and sniff it, you'll smell the bitter, almondlike odor of cyanide. Some people can't smell cyanide, but the bugs' main enemies—birds—can. The bright colors are also a warning to birds to leave the bug alone.

Kiss of death

The Sydney funnel-web spider is one of the few spiders whose bite can kill a human, although deaths are rare. It bites aggressively and repeatedly, and its fangs can pierce a fingernail or puncture a shoe. The venom contains a cocktail of nerve poisons that can cause unbearable pain, twitching, vomiting, coma, and death.

Prickly peril

Never touch a spiked or hairy caterpillar. The spikes and hairs are designed to break into needle-sharp fragments that pierce your skin and inject a pain-inducing venom. Caterpillars can also steal chemical weapons from plants. They feed on poisonous plants and store the toxic chemicals in their bodies for protection.

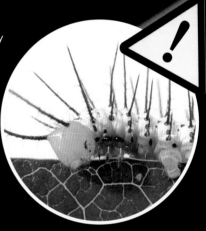

A sting in the tail

The fat-tailed scorpion of North Africa kills more people than any other scorpion. Its venom contains nerve poisons that spread from the wound to affect the whole body. This is what can happen if you get stung: rapid breathing, weakness, sweating, frothing at the mouth, blurred vision, rolling eyes, vomiting, diarrea, chest pain, seizures, and death.

Take the pain

The bullet ant of Central America has the most painful sting of any insect. The searing pain lasts 24 hours and is said to be like a bullet piercing the body. Rainforest tribes use the ants in a ceremony of manhood. Boys wear a woven sleeve in which the ants are trapped and must endure dozens of stings to prove their courage.

 **DEANLY** **CORROSIVE** ! **IRRITATING**

Friend OR

Wasps might have a nasty sting, but they are efficient predators and kill huge numbers of pests, such as caterpillars. Definitely friends.

Honeybees give us honey and wax, and they also carry pollen from flower to flower, helping crops to produce fruit and seeds. So they are mostly friends… except the dreaded African variety, which isn't very friendly at all.

Ladybugs are also friendly predators. They prey on the tiny greenflies that infest garden plants. Some people buy ladybugs and release them in greenhouses to control pests.

Don't panic! I'm gonna get that pesky fly!

Spiders kill billions of pests and disease-carrying insects, especially flies, and they never lay a fang on our plants or buildings.

Bumblebees are great pollinators, dutifully buzzing from flower to flower and so helping plants to fruit. They are especially good at pollinating greenhouse plants like tomatoes.

I'm a foe because I spread disease, but I can also be a friend and help recycle things.

FOE?

Many people think **insects** and **spiders** are just *pests* that infest our homes and gardens. In fact, a lot of them actually help us. So who are our **friends** and who are our **foes?**

Carpenter ants dig hollows in wood for their nests, and they don't care whether the wood is part of a tree or an important part of your home. At night they sneak out to raid your kitchen for sweet or greasy foods.

Cabbage white butterflies may be pretty, but their caterpillars aren't popular with gardeners. They eat nearly all the same vegetables as us: cauliflowers, cabbages, sprouts, broccoli, radishes, kale, mustard…

Fee, fie, **foe**, fum…

Termites don't just burrow into the wood in homes—they eat it. They do it all out of sight, so they can totally wreck a house before you discover them.

Greenflies suck the sap out of all kinds of plants and multiply at a phenomenal rate by giving birth to clones without having to mate. They also squirt out sugary excrement that causes mold.

Flour beetles find their way into kitchen cupboards and feast on all kinds of dried food—from flour and pasta to crackers and powdered milk. Most definitely foes!

Hmmm, moldy old flour—my favorite!

Colorado beetles once lived only in the Rocky Mountains, but they have now spread across the world as a pest of potato plants. The larvae devour the leaves and ruin the crop.

What is the **deadliest** animal in the **world?**

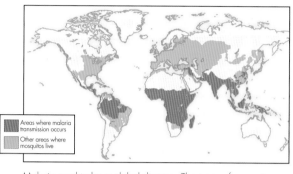

Malaria used to be a global disease. The types of mosquito that can spread the malaria germs are found nearly everywhere, except deserts and very cold places. In the 20th century, many countries succeeded in wiping out the germs (though not the mosquitos). However, malaria is still common in tropical countries, as are the other mosquito-borne diseases listed below.

Before supper...

Meet the humble female mosquito, the cause of nearly half of all human deaths in history. As she drives her piercing mouthparts deep into your skin to suck your blood, she can also inject microscopic germs that cause a fatal disease. Malaria is the most common—it kills more than half a million people a year. But it's not the only one. Travel in a malaria zone and you run the risk of getting any of the nasty diseases below.

Female mosquitos suck human blood so that they can make eggs. Males don't bite and are so small and insignificant that you've probably never seen one. You're most likely to get bitten in the evening when the air is still—most mosquitos rest during daylight and they can't stand moving air. As the female drinks, her abdomen swells up with blood and turns red. Her saliva contains a painkiller so you don't feel the bite... until it's too late.

... after supper

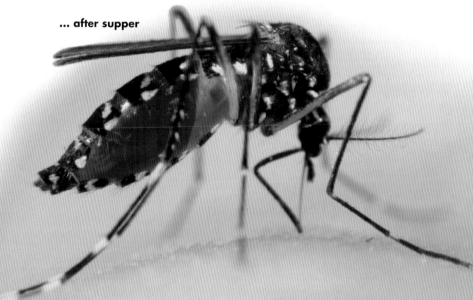

What *mosquitos* can do to you

DENGUE FEVER causes a rash of red spots on your skin and terrible pains in your joints and bones.
YELLOW FEVER turns your vomit black and your skin yellow. Then you go into a coma and may die.
WEST NILE VIRUS spreads through your blood into your brain, which then swells up and often kills you.
MALARIA produces a raging fever that flares up repeatedly every two or three days. Often fatal.
ELEPHANTIASIS makes your legs swell up like elephants' legs because of tiny worms, spread by mosquitos, that burrow into your skin.

74

Malaria germs breed inside **red blood cells** (shown here magnified).

In 1790, **10%** of Philadelphia's population was wiped out in a single summer by **yellow fever.**

Malaria can kill you in **1 day** or can stay hidden in your body for **30 years.**

500 million people catch malaria every year.

1 in **5** people who catch the most severe form of malaria die.

1 in **17** of all people alive today will die because of a mosquito bite.

22,000 French workers died building the Panama Canal because of **malaria** and **yellow fever.**

Every **12** seconds a child dies of **malaria.**

More than **half** of the French emperor Napoleon's army was killed by yellow fever when he invaded Haiti in 1802.

Malaria doesn't just make humans sick—it makes mosquitos sick too.

RECORD BREAKERS

Migration
Some animals embark on long journeys, called migrations, to find new homes. Arthropods can migrate thousands of miles by riding on the wind. The desert locust (*Schistocerca gregaria*) of Africa regularly travels vast distances in windblown swarms across the Sahara Desert as it searches for food. In 1988, a swarm flew all the way across the Atlantic Ocean by riding on powerful tropical winds that later generated a hurricane. The locusts landed in the South American countries of Suriname and Guyana and on the Virgin Islands.

longest fastest tallest highest loudest smallest

Longest INSECT

Phobaeticus chani, a stick insect from the jungles of Borneo, is a staggering 22 in (57cm) long—wider than the pages of this book when open.

Fastest on land

The American cockroach is the official holder of this record, with a top speed of 3½ mph (5.4 kph). But scientific reports suggest an Australian tiger beetle may be capable of 5½ mph (8.96 kph)— nearly twice as fast.

Tallest HOME

African termite mounds, at up to 42 ft (13 m) tall, are the tallest buildings made by any non-human animal. If we made buildings as big in proportion to our bodies, they would be 3 miles (4.5 km) tall.

Best JUMPER

The froghopper, or spittle bug, is the high-jumper of the insect world, capable of reaching 28 in (70 cm) high. The froghopper is only ¼ in (6.3 mm) long and so this is the equivalent of a human leaping on to a 55-story building in a single bound.

Philip McCabe stood for over 2 hours covered in 60 lb (27 kg) of bees and was stung only seven times.

Largest BUTTERFLY

Queen Alexandra's birdwing of Papua New Guinea is the biggest butterfly, with a wingspan of 11 in (28 cm). The biggest moth is the Atlas moth from Malaysia, with a wingspan of 1 ft (30 cm).

Most babies
Social insects have more babies than any other arthropod. A queen honeybee lays 200,000 eggs a year and lives for four years, so she can produce 800,000 offspring in her lifetime. But the record holder is the queen termite. Laying eggs at an average rate of 21 a minute, she produces 30,000 eggs a day. During her lifetime, she can have 100 million offspring.

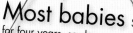

laziest youngest oldest smallest loudest

Shortest LIFE

Mayflies have the shortest adult lives of insects, lasting only a day or so—enough time to mate. Aphids take the shortest time to reproduce—they can give birth just seven days after being born.

Smallest SPIDER

Patu digua of Colombia is the world's smallest spider, at only 0.014 in (3.7 mm) long. However, other arachnids, such as mites, are smaller. The smallest insect is a fairy wasp, just 0.005 in (0.14 mm) long.

LONGEST hibernation

Yucca moths have been known to spend 19 years hibernating as pupas before emerging as adult moths. Many insects are capable of entering a state of hibernation (called diapause) to avoid cold or dry weather.

LARGEST WEB

Darwin's bark spiders in Madagascar build giant orb webs up to 10 ft (3 m) wide, with draglines stretching 82 ft (25 m). They catch insects such as mayflies and dragonflies.

oldest youngest laziest smelliest

Fastest BUG

Hawkmoths are among the fastest fliers (along with botflies, horseflies, and some butterflies), able to maintain an airspeed of 24 mph (39 kph). Some dragonflies, however, can achieve 36 mph (58 kph) for short bursts.

FASTEST wing beat

Forcipomyia—a kind of midge—can beat its wings 1,046 times a second. The wings are powered by the fastest muscles known to exist.

Biggest BEE BEARD

Philip McCabe of Ireland risked being stung to death when he covered himself with 200,000 honeybees in June 2005 in an attempt to beat the world record for having the "largest bee beard." The current record is 350,000 bees, held by Mark Biancaniello of California.

LOUDEST insect

Male cicadas can sing at volumes of up to 109 decibels, which is almost as loud as a jackhammer. The songs are audible from ½ mile (0.5 km) away.

Longest life

Wood-boring beetles can survive as larvae inside wood for 35 to 50 years before emerging as adults. Queen termites have the longest lifespan of any insect, surviving for up to 60 years as head of their colony.

highest fastest longest

GLOSSARY

Abdomen the part of an animal's body that contains digestive and reproductive organs. An insect's abdomen is at the rear of the body.

Antennae (feelers) long sensory organs on the head of an arthropod. They feel, taste, and smell objects as well as sensing vibrations.

Arachnid a member of the class Arachnida, a particular branch of the arthropod family tree. Arachnids have eight legs and include spiders, scorpions, ticks, and mites.

Arthropod an animal with jointed legs (or appendages) and an exoskeleton.

Caterpillar the wingless larva of a butterfly or moth.

Chrysalis the pupa of a butterfly. Chysalises have a hard outer case for protection.

Cocoon the protective silk case around the pupa of a moth.

Colony a large group of animals living closely together. Social insects such as bees and ants live in colonies.

Compound eye an eye made up of hundreds of tiny units, each of which makes a separate image.

Crustacean a member of the superclass Crustacea, a particular branch of the arthropod family tree. Most crustaceans live in water. Crabs, shrimp, lobsters, and wood lice are crustaceans.

Digestive system consists of organs of the body that break down food so that it can be absorbed.

Exoskeleton the outer skeleton (cuticle) of an arthropod.

Fang tooth that can deliver digestive juices or venom.

Gill organ used to breathe underwater.

Grub the larva of a beetle, wasp, or bee.

Haltere one of a pair of drumstick-shaped structures on a fly's body that beat with the wings to aid balance.

Hive a structure that houses a bee colony.

Insect a member of the class Insecta, a particular branch of the arthropod family tree. Insects have three main body parts and six legs.

Invertebrate an animal without a backbone. All arthropods are invertebrates, as are worms, snails, slugs, and many sea creatures.

Larva an immature form of an insect. Larvae look very different from the adults. Caterpillars, for example, are the larvae of butterflies.

Metamorphosis the dramatic change that occurs when a larva (an immature insect) turns into an adult. Caterpillars metamorphose when they change into butterflies.

Migration a long journey by an animal to find a new place to live. Some animals migrate regularly every year.

Molt the shedding of an arthropod's exoskeleton. Arthropods have to molt to grow.

Nectar a sugary liquid made by flowers to attract pollinating insects.

Nymph an immature form of an insect that looks similar to the adult. Nymphs grow into adults by molting several times.

Parasite a small organism that lives on or inside the body of a bigger organism, feeding on it while it is still alive.

Pedipalps a pair of small armlike appendages on the head of an arachnid, on each side of the mouth.

Pollen a powdery substance, made in flowers, that contains male sex cells. When pollen is transferred to the female part of a flower, the flower can produce a seed or fruit.

Pollination the transfer of pollen from male organs in flowers to female organs. Pollination is a very important stage in the reproduction of plants.

Predator an animal that kills and eats other animals.

Prey an animal that is killed and eaten by a predator.

Proboscis a long, flexible snout or mouthpart. A butterfly uses a proboscis (also called a tongue) to suck nectar from flowers.

Pupa the resting stage in the life cycle of an insect, during which a larva is tranformed into an adult by the process of metamorphosis.

Sap a liquid that transports nutrients around plants.

Silk a tough, stretchy fiber produced by spiders to make webs or by moth caterpillars to make cocoons.

Solitary alone.

Species a type of organism. The members of a species can breed with each other. Some species have successfully bred with other species.

Spiracle a hole in the exoskeleton of an arthropod that lets air circulate through the body.

Thorax the central body part of an insect, between the head and abdomen.

Venom a poisonous substance in an animal's bite or sting.

Giant weta

Rhinoceros beetle grub

Bluebottles

INDEX

Wood ants

Longhorn beetle

CREDITS

The publisher would like to thank the following for their assistance in the preparation of this book: Sonia Yooshing for editorial assistance and Riti Sodhi for design assistance.